A Dialogue on Christianity

A Dialogue on
CHRISTIANITY

ERNEST MILNER AND FRANK HOERNER

iUniverse, Inc.
New York   Bloomington

A Dialogue on Christianity

iUniverse books may be ordered through booksellers or by contacting:

iUniverse
1663 Liberty Drive
Bloomington, IN 47403
www.iuniverse.com
1-800-Authors (1-800-288-4677)

Because of the dynamic nature of the Internet, any Web addresses or links contained in this book may have changed since publication and may no longer be valid. The views expressed in this work are solely those of the authors and do not necessarily reflect the views of the publisher, and the publisher hereby disclaims any responsibility for them.

ISBN: 978-1-4502-4924-9 (sc)
ISBN: 978-1-4502-4925-6 (ebk)

Printed in the United States of America

iUniverse rev. date: 08/26/2010

CONTENTS

PREFACE

The positive signs that Christianity is alive and well are many. Most churches reflect the teachings of Christ through their outreach to the less fortunate, their support to churches in third world countries, and the enthusiasm and uplifting nature of the worship services. While differences in theological emphasis have resulted in conflicts and an ever growing number of denominations, as a total group they generally join together as brothers and sisters in Christ, and see themselves as part of His family. The current status of the Church provides good reason to be optimistic about the future, but there are always challenges to be faced.

Given the importance of what we call religion, with all that it entails, including an acknowledgement of Almighty God; the origin and purpose of life; our accepted Christian/Judaic values and culture; our personal relationship with Christ; our soul and the prospect for eternal life, you might think that most people would seek out and eagerly follow the lessons taught in the Bible and through the teachings of the Church. And yet, the statistics seem to show that while many people claim to be Christians, a much smaller percent actually embrace the Church as a focal point of their daily lives.

There are many studies that help to shed light upon the current state of the Church. It is likely that among the findings is the fact that being a practicing Christian is not easy. Most people, when faced with a choice will seek the one that gives immediate pleasure and requires the least commitment. It's easy to justify that view since it's the road most often traveled, and the one that society increasingly encourages. An opinion that is often expressed points to recent generations being indoctrinated with the very questionable concept that the Constitution of the United States limits religion in the public domain, and relegates it to something less than a common bond among the majority of the people. The role in our society of marriage and family has also been diminished. The ease and prevalence of abortion has put into question the sanctity of life, and the hand of God in the creation of life. The pursuit and abundance of material things and ease of pleasure have reduced the importance of moral values and commitment to God. The growth of technology has brought forth an unwarranted increase in the belief that man is the ultimate power and capable of doing whatever has to be done. So, in the minds of many, God is no longer relevant or needed. But there is another more subtle factor. As people look at the Christian community, both within the United States and around the world, they often see differences in beliefs, friction, and a general lack of understanding of just what it means to be a Christian.

For the most part, Churches do well in professing issues of faith, but given the nature of an increasingly cynical and sophisticated population there may not be as much done in the area of learning about Christianity past the elementary level. While the title of the well known book by Robert Fulghum, "All I Really Need to Know I Learned in Kindergarten" may well be true in many aspects of life, the really important lessons of life aren't available to most of us until we're old enough to ask the right questions and to absorb some profound truths. When learning about Christianity is pursued, it is often done in small Bible study groups which, while extremely well motivated and worthwhile, are without the oversight or teaching that can only come from someone who not only encompasses the faith but also has the level of knowledge that can only be obtained through theological training. Indeed, many of the answers to the questions that grow out of these Bible study sessions relate to the importance of faith, but that too calls for the consideration and response from someone with formal education and knowledge of the Bible.

As we pursue a study of the Bible and how to be practicing Christians, we might well consider ourselves students. In that capacity it's common, if not essential, to ask questions. At the elementary level many, if not most, people learn the books of the Bible and the basic facts of Christianity, but as we proceed in our quest for faith and understanding, it becomes necessary to go more deeply into what lessons are intended to be provided through the Bible. We aren't likely to come upon the same people or events that are portrayed in the Bible, but if we understand the intent of our reading we'll be able to extrapolate and more closely apply the lessons taught by Christ, and also live our lives in a manner more pleasing to our heavenly Father.

What follows in this book, with questions by Ernest Milner and authoritative responses by Frank Hoerner, is an attempt to bring forth thoughtful issues that might well be considered by small Bible study groups who are seeking to better understand Christianity. Generally, through the process of questioning and obtaining increased knowledge, the faith of most people grows stronger. Hopefully this humble effort that relates the questions to Biblical references and insights by Frank Hoerner will help to bring forth that end, and those who read it will have a better understanding of Christianity.

INTRODUCTION

As a young teenager attending both Sunday school and Confirmation classes in the Episcopal Church, I learned to recite the books of the Bible, gathered the basic facts that serve as the foundation of Christianity, and was exposed to the liturgy of the Church. It was by all accounts an elementary education akin to knowing how to read basic words, but without any real understanding of the underlying meaning and not much about how it should be applied in the course of daily living.

As is true with most people, the years that followed were consumed by essential duties, school, and military service, marriage, raising children and pursuing a career. Fortunately, over the course of those years, and in interaction with others, celebrating holidays, and being exposed to both happy and difficult events, I came face to face with the realization that religion had not risen to the priority in my life that was warranted. In short, my life reflected that of millions of other people who claim to be Christians, but lacked the depth of commitment to make it a reality. When retirement provided the time to reflect upon what I had missed, I sought to listen more closely to the sermons of our Lutheran pastors, read more, and joined two small Bible study groups with a sincere thirst to fill the void in my knowledge and to strengthen my faith.

The Bible is often considered the most important book in the world, but it's not a novel that can be read quickly, nor can it be easily understood. On the extremes, there are those who say that you should not be inquisitive when reading the Bible, just accept the words as they appear and let faith dictate your understanding. Then, there are those who look for logic, facts, historical proof of the stories and lessons that come from the Bible. But, many find that they are not part of the two extremes, rather they prefer to enhance their faith by seeking what it means to be a Christian. Many would agree that an intellectual pursuit of hard historical evidence to support each story of the Bible would be difficult. But, a reasonable person might well look at the world as it currently exists some two thousand years after the Lord walked among us and see what a giant and positive effect He has had on mankind. You need not see photographs, images, statues or listen to recordings of the time to see the influence that Christ had on those with whom he had contact. Whatever happened during that period made such a lasting impression that it changed the world and mankind forever.

I cannot overstate the value that I found in participating over several years in informal Bible study groups. However, in the typical student fashion, each session raised questions. In time I came to realize that without a teacher trained in theology, whatever discussion or response that followed my questions could not necessarily be counted upon to be accurate or complete. As I found myself accumulating questions and giving thought to putting them in a form to share with others, I also started to consider how I wanted to go about finding the right person to provide the answers. At the outset, I made a mental note to avoid any attempt to influence the nature of the responses. There would be no contrived agreement, no "stacking the deck" or pre-agreed upon rules to help bring forth answers that I would be happy to hear. But, rather I decided to seek an objective, academically sound reaction that was not provided in the form of a sermon, dogmatic or reflective of any one denomination. As most people would do, I initially gravitated toward the arena in which I felt most comfortable, the Lutheran or Episcopal clergy. But, as I thought more about it, I decided that it wasn't comfort that I was seeking, but rather a dialogue with someone that I personally knew, trusted and respected for his judgment, wisdom, experience and knowledge. In addition, from a practical stand-point, I also considered that a retired person would be an asset since the project would require a significant commitment of time and effort. Also, while I recognized that no two people, no matter how well educated in the Bible and Christianity, would answer every question exactly the same, I set some criteria to help ensure that the eventual responses would be credible, consistent with the teachings of Christ and a map to guide me and those who read what follows toward a better understanding of what it means to be a Christian.

Finally, the light went on and I remembered my former associate in the Department of Justice, Frank Hoerner. While it had been a number of years since Frank and I had seen each other, we once shared the common experience of developing a challenging national program that emanated from the Office of the President and was surprisingly sparse in its guidance or direction. In the years that followed I got to see Frank from the best of perspectives. He was conspicuous in his sound judgment, wisdom, integrity, and intellect. In addition, on the more private side of our relationship I knew that he was a former Roman Catholic priest who had impressive credentials as a religious leader. After leaving the priesthood, he married and was the father of two children. While he no longer wore the priestly collar, he continued to live his life as a disciple of Christ, and those of us who knew him also knew that he was an example of what a Christian should be. In addition, I knew that we shared the ability to communicate well and neither of us would have trouble understanding what was being said, or in accepting each others values and beliefs.

From the moment that Frank picked-up his phone and heard my request to co-author this book, he was totally onboard, and with the understanding that he would have the hard part – the "heavy lifting". With incredible enthusiasm and focus, he worked full time in addressing the responses to my questions. While it may be hard for the reader to visualize, in the weeks that followed, we had no direct discussion other than by e-mail. Frank just "pumped out" the responses without the need for clarification of the intended meaning of my questions. He understood, and I had the privilege of absorbing his responses. It was truly a student-teacher experience, not a sermon, but rather a spontaneous but well considered, honest, and thoughtful series of responses. While some of his comments were not what I would have expected, they were what I sought - provocative, honest, personal, from the heart, mind, and his academic background. Finally, when we finished the first cut of the content, we spoke on the phone about three times to review what we had done, fix a few misspellings, consider any miscommunication or other problems, and discuss how we would move to the next stage and get our thoughts in print. The conversations were short, easy, light, and a reflection of what we initially intended, which was to engage in a dialogue on some very weighty issues.

It's obviously not practical for Frank to sit-in on the thousands of small Bible study groups that meet informally around the country on a regular basis. But, it's my hope that the wisdom and teaching that he provides in this book is as helpful to others as it has been for me.

To help the reader in differentiating between our comments, we decided that Frank's would follow immediately after mine, and his would be in italics.

Frank, would you like to add your own introductory comments?

Ernie, I was very surprised and honored to receive your phone call telling me about this book and inviting me to become a part of it.

I don't consider myself a scholar. I am a Christian who has had a wonderful opportunity to study and be ordained a Catholic priest. I do not pretend that my responses are the only way to respond, but they are representative of my belief and understanding. I have tried to respond to each question with my deepest honesty and commitment to the faith in Jesus Christ that I believe in today. I fully realize that I am not where I was in my faith five or ten years ago, or perhaps, not even last year! And that is good, because faith is not something stagnant! If it doesn't grow, it dies!

I don't expect the reader to agree with all my responses, because each reader may be at a different place than I am in his faith. That does not mean that either of us is better than the other; or that one is right and the other is wrong. It just means we should recognize there is a difference, respect that difference, and remember that the good Lord accepts us where we are as long as we are trying to be where we think He wants us to be. We don't even have to be where He wants us to be; just where <u>we think</u> He wants us to be! All I ask the reader to do is to consider my response to each question and tweak it if need be, then give his own response.

If I may, I would like to tell you a little bit about myself so that the readers get a better glimpse of who I am. I grew up in a very Roman Catholic family - the eleventh of thirteen children. From the time I was in third grade, I always wanted to be a priest. So at the age of fourteen, I entered the seminary and after thirteen years of prayer and studies, I was ordained in June, 1962. I worked in Puerto Rico and the Dominican Republic. Then in 1969 after prayer and seeking counsel and with a dispensation from Rome, I left the active ministry and married my wonderful wife, Alfonsina.

Adjusting to a drastic change in life wasn't easy, but I have been more blessed than I deserved with the people I have met and the opportunities given me. Eventually I landed a job with the Federal

Government in Washington, DC. One of the best and most fortunate job opportunities came my way when I was selected with one other person to work on a special Presidential initiative under your leadership, Ernie. I'm sure you remember that well!

You were the boss, but we never felt like you were. I could not have found a person who was more kind, gentle, and understanding than you were. (That may embarrass you, but those are my feelings.) You remember that our assignment was to develop a program with another federal agency. Though our agency played the lead role and provided the funding, you never lorded it over the other agency, nor tried to ensure that our agency had the upper hand. You were most conciliatory, fair-minded, and generous in safeguarding the other agency's integrity by showing them a deep-seated respect for their ideas and efforts. And that impressed me!

Though I knew you to be a Christian, I really didn't know how deeply your faith governed your life. You did try to recruit me as a Chaplin in the Navy Reserve, but I was just one year over the age limit. That should have given me a clue! But there were other clues which I have just come to realize now since you have invited me to join you in producing this book. I always remember you as being very even-tempered. You never showed any anger or disgust, but were always positive and reassuring and often played the devil's advocate defending the other agency when our fellow-worker and I were critical of them. I can honestly say that I never saw you angry. And now I know that back some thirty years ago, your conduct was just a reflection of that deep faith which you show through your questions. I think you would have made a good minister yourself!

One last comment, Ernie. God is spirit and spirit has no gender. But English has no appropriate pronouns to refer to God. While most people will use "He" and "Him", my preference would be "S/He" and "Him/Her" in order to recognize this language deficiency.

However, this choice sounds rather cumbersome in any lengthy writing. Therefore, I will conform to the more commonly accepted use of the masculine pronouns to refer to God, asking the reader to be mindful of my comment above.

DEDICATION

**To those who seek to be closer to God
and enhance their faith through informal
group meetings to study the Bible.**

Part One

Our Relationship With God

OUR RELATIONSHIP WITH GOD

It's been said that the closest a person will ever be to God while on earth is the moment that he's born. Almost immediately thereafter, he's affected by all the human qualities and necessities to survive in a less than perfect world, including the immediate need for food, water, and nurturing. Eventually that learning quietly segues into the development of behavior that in his mind helps him to achieve his goals. Success breeds success, so when he finds how best to obtain gratification and pleasure he seeks to take that route.

Those fortunate enough to be exposed to God along the way generally maintain a balance, a moral compass, and an understanding that their life is intended to have a purpose beyond their own self interest. But, all too often, the road to maturity has detours, rocks, and obstacles that interfere with the ability to see the purpose for which we were born – the glorification of God.

If left alone, most people will flounder. They'll follow the course of least resistance, the easiest, the most physically rewarding, and the most self-centered. Some people eventually come across what we might consider a worldly angel. When they least expect it, people often, without any effort on their part, encounter a Christian who, while not necessarily intending to reach out and affect the life of some one else does just that. Often the encounter is by example, or at a time when the other person is in need, and when exposed to the light of Christ is effected and starts to re-evaluate his life.

Few if any, people are born into a certain and absolute life style that will bring forth a relationship with God. It's most often when a person is moving through life, encountering all its challenges and his weaknesses that he finds that his ability alone is not enough to accomplish what is important, or how he can best achieve the maximum benefit from his life on earth Eventually, many, but unfortunately not all, people find that the purpose, the goal, and the only important thing in life is their relationship with God.

Frank, do you have any comments that you would like to add?

Ernie, I don't know what led you to choose the divisions of this book into the four parts that you have chosen, but, I don't think that you could have chosen four more important areas of our lives to wonder and converse about than God, our neighbor, the Bible, and the Church. The materialist – the one who is concerned about anything but the spiritual, the hereafter, or God – unfortunately will not likely so much as glance at this book. But you have shown a very deep spiritual interest into the most important areas of our lives.

St. Augustine once said, "Our hearts were made for you, O Lord, and they will not rest until they rest in You." By your questions you show this same restlessness Augustine knew.

What is "Our Relationship with God?" I am not naïve enough to think that I have come very close to adequately explaining that answer. God is too powerful, too omnipotent, too all-knowing, and too full of awe for any human to even try to pretend to comprehend the smallest portion of His infinity, eternalness, graciousness, kindness, forgiveness, or total and unconditional love.

And yet, I do not believe that with all His majesty, He does not expect us poor human beings not to wonder. Of course, God does not need our wondering, or our thinking, or our questioning about who He is. He is God! And we can only speak as humans speak regardless of how inadequate that may be.

And so some of your questions, and many of my responses will fall very short of who this Being is. When we finally meet our Maker, I hope He will not embarrass us too much by showing how far off we were from knowing Him as He really is by our poor attempts of knowing Him with our inadequate questions and more terribly inadequate answers.

What I have attempted to do in this first section is to answer your questions as best as I understood them and provide you with my simple understanding from my current spiritual point of view. That is where I am now. I haven't always been here, and I can not assure you that I will be here tomorrow. Hopefully I will grow beyond these limits, and I hope that you will too.

PART ONE

OUR RELATIONSHIP WITH GOD

QUESTIONS

&

RESPONSES

QUESTION #1

Some say that there is nothing that we can do to earn salvation. It is a gift from God – it's Grace – bought by Christ's death on the cross. On the other hand, there are those who profess to be confident of their salvation because they believe in Christ. In addition, they conclude that those who have not accepted Christ as their personal savior can not enter the kingdom of God. If so, does that amount to a requirement that must be earned? Does it therefore contradict the belief that salvation is solely in the hands of the Lord and based on Grace? In addition, does it conflict with the exclusive authority of God to make the decision of who can, or will, enter heaven? Some people proclaim that unless you know Jesus you can not enter the kingdom of God. What would be the definition of and criteria for, knowing Jesus? If God is (as is accepted by Christians) the almighty sovereign, is it appropriate for us to determine who meets with His approval and on what basis? Does the statement of Paul in Romans 9:16, "So then it depends not on human will or exertion, but on God, who has mercy", apply to that thought and question?

RESPONSE #1

Salvation can not be earned! It is a pure gift of God given out of the abundance of His love through Christ's death on the cross. So there is nothing that we can do to "earn" salvation. We can not pray our way into salvation, we can not earn it by doing good works or deeds, nor can we gain it by living a good, moral life. Just believing in Christ doesn't assure anyone of salvation either. We humans tend to see things from a dual vision, i.e., one or the other rather than "both and", and this latter concept is very foreign to our western way of thinking. So we see "the belief that salvation is solely in the hands of the Lord and at the same time based on Grace" as a contradiction – one or the other. Our minds are very limited and no one can conceive of the mind of God. So while something may seem as a contradiction (Christ being both human and divine), it is entirely possible to be anything but a contradiction. What it may well be is our limited human capacity to comprehend "the mystery of God" (Colossians 1:24-29). This entire question of salvation – who will be saved and how, and why - sometimes seems to bog down Christians trying to understand the mind of God. Yes, I believe that the statement of Paul in Romans 9:16, "So then it depends not on human will or exertion, but on God, who has mercy", applies to this thought.

The story of St. Augustine comes to mind as he walked upon the sea shore trying to understand the mystery of the Trinity. He came upon a little child who had dug a hole in the sand and was pouring water from the sea with a sea shell into the little hole. Augustine asked the child what he was doing and he explained that he was going to empty the sea into the little hole. Augustine told the child he could never do that. Then the child told Augustine that neither would he ever understand the Trinity. To have a better understanding of this issue, we should read Romans 9:15, as well. "He (God) says to Moses, "I will show mercy to whomever I wish; I will have pity on whomever I wish." Salvation depends on God! It is our responsibility to live our lives in conformity with His will and trust in God's word.

You ask, "What would be the definition of, and criteria for, knowing Jesus?" My definition of Jesus is "love" – both of God and neighbor; the criteria would be how one lives His daily life. If any one is trying, no matter how many times she or he fails, to follow Jesus in the every day events of one's life, that person meets my criteria for knowing Christ.

QUESTION #2

The practice of prayer, our primary means of communicating with God, is not always viewed consistently. Some say that it should be done quietly (in the closet); others say that it should openly express our faith and glorification of God. Some say that it should not be a "wish list" that would make our lives more pleasant and comfortable, while others regularly seek God's intervention for the daily functions of life. What guidance can you offer?

RESPONSE #2

What is prayer? Many will say "conversation with God" or "lifting the mind and heart to God." Is it verbal conversation, like human talk? Is it written words in a prayer book that we repeat, or is it some formula, like the "Hail Mary" or the "Our Father", or is it our own words and thoughts as we go about the day asking God for forgiveness, help, guidance, etc. Yes, it's all of the above, but for many it means only some formula or words that they say. Prayer to me is consciously putting your self in God's presence.

Think of two lovers. They call each other every day; they try to see each other as often as they can. If apart for any length of time, they may write letters or send cards besides their frequent calls. But even when they are not in "actual" communication with each other, they are most probably thinking of each other and planning things, or recalling past encounters. They spend many, many moments of the day just thinking and even day dreaming about the other person. Yes, they are in communication with the other in their minds and thoughts and in their hearts. We could call this latter type of communication "mental conversation" for that is what it really is. And that is also a form of prayer called "mental prayer" or "meditation".

Or think of a mother sitting along the bedside of her sick child all during the night just watching and caring for her little one! Is she present to her child? Is she in communication with her little sick one?

Now let's apply this to God. We can mentally converse with God throughout the entire day as we work, eat, or go to bed. Even just the thought of God, or the thought "I want to pray" or "I should pray" is a prayer in itself. We can read the Bible or any spiritual reading material that makes us mentally aware of God or of improving our own spiritual life. All of these things are prayers and probably of more use to us than formulas. Remember, God doesn't need our prayers; we do. Our prayers aren't going to change God. They are meant to change us; to give us the proper disposition that we need to have before God.

When we pray we should recall Matthew 7:7 and pray with that same attitude. "Ask, and you will receive. Seek, and you will find. Knock, and it will be opened to you…If you, with all your sins, know how to give your children what is good, how much more will your heavenly Father give good things to anyone who asks Him!"

I think all the various practices of prayer that you refer to have a place in our lives depending on the particular circumstances in which we find ourselves. Certainly I highly recommend daily prayers as we move from one activity to the other. It's a way of deepening our consciousness of God's presence in our lives and makes us aware of our need and dependence on Him.

QUESTION #3

Some question whether you can know God only through Christ. One point of view is based on the Old Testament which indicates that Abraham, Moses, and a number of others knew God before Jesus came among us. The other view is based on the New Testament which indicates that the exclusive way to know God is through Christ. How should we view that issue?

RESPONSE #3

Obviously we can not say that the "exclusive" way to know God is through Christ since the Old Testament shows that Abraham, Moses and others knew God before Christ came. One view in understanding the New Testament is that Paul and others are preaching to those to whom they have made Christ known. To insist that God is only known through Christ puts us back into the idea of salvation again. What about those hundreds of thousands of souls who never had the opportunity through no fault of their own to know Christ? Certainly an all-loving and all-merciful God is not going to punish those thousands of souls.

For our own happiness we have to be satisfied that there are and will be many things we will never know. We are finite. Our intellect does not know everything – and this is especially true of the spiritual world. This is just one of the many answers we do not know. Our duty is to love God by trying to live our lives according to His will. While many questions of this type are interesting for a theological discussion, we should not let them derail our faith or weaken our trust in God. Trust these other souls to the mercy and justice of God. You recall Christ's parable of the laborers in the vineyard (Matthew 20:1-16). I often think of this parable as applying in some way to this question about those who didn't know Christ through no fault of their own. I'm not sure it applies exactly, but the same thought is there.

When we come to meet our Creator face to face, I doubt very much whether He is going to ask us what religion we belonged to, or which Church we attended, or who was our pastor, etc., etc. I firmly believe our Creator will ask each one of us – regardless of our religion – this one simple question: "Did you live your life the way I revealed myself to YOU?"

QUESTION #4

We learn as Christians that it is not what we do that leads to salvation since salvation is a gift from God through Christ – Grace. But, there also seems to be a personal responsibility that is placed upon us to be obedient to the will of God. Free will is not a license to do whatever we want without consequences. How should we balance these two factors?

RESPONSE #4

Certainly we must be grateful for the gifts of salvation - grace, and, free will, and recognize that they are two different and distinct gifts. No one is absolutely sure of his own salvation until he eventually reaches heaven. Many people from different faiths often speak about themselves as "already saved" since they have surrendered their lives to Christ and made a firm commitment to follow Him. They presume that there is never a chance of turning back, no chance of their failure to stick to their convictions until the end. When you think of it, the common view that conversion is a one-time event is rather puzzling. Why do members of Alcohol Anonymous keep attending those daily meetings? I wonder if there is anyone who does not know someone who has wavered in their commitment to Christ. It can happen to anyone of us and no one should be so presumptuous as to think that it could not. Remember, "The spirit is willing but nature is weak" (Matthew 26:41).

It is precisely because of our free will (to do as we please) that we should be extremely cautious about our assurance of salvation. We are continually and constantly battered daily by all sorts of temptations, worldly allurements, and questionable pleasures and the subtleness with which these are presented have laid a devious trap for many who seek the highroad of goodness. Scripture tells us, "Stay sober and alert. Your opponent the devil is prowling like a roaring lion looking for someone to devour" (1 Peter 5:8).

QUESTION #5

The Bible speaks to the issue of sex, and certainly it's a strong force in the world. But, is too much emphasis placed on the dangers of lust? Many enjoy the attraction of the opposite sex and don't see them as a threat, or the lurking devil; and yet, so often it is an issue that is associated with sin. How should we view our relationship and interaction with members of the opposite sex?

RESPONSE # 5

Is too much emphasis placed on the dangers of lust? I couldn't help but think of how frequently lust has brought down so many sports figures, movie actors, politicians, even clergy, and so many others.

The natural attraction for the opposite sex is a gift from God and sex itself is one of God's most powerful and beautiful gifts if used properly. It is in sharing God's gifts with one another in marriage that a man and woman can become co-creators with God in bringing new beings into existence. That is an awesome privilege. "Be fertile and multiply;"(Genesis 1:28). We should appreciate members of the opposite sex and respect them as equals and partners whether in marriage, friendship, Church, at work, and in every part of our society and recognize their God-given different gifts, talents, abilities, and charm.

St. Peter tells us in his first letter (1Peter 3:7) "You, husbands, too, must show consideration for those who share your lives. Treat women with respect..." Our U. S. Constitution states that "all men" - EVERYONE including women - "are created equal."

QUESTION #6

If a person is born without the benefit of nurturing, and is by necessity consumed by the need to survive in a hostile environment – one which excludes Christianity and embraces sin and crime, are they held to the same standards as those of us who were fortunate enough to grow-up in the Christian faith?

RESPONSE # 6

I firmly believe each of us will be judged by the opportunities that have been offered to us. If we humans can have compassion for a poor, uneducated person not knowing what is expected of him, how much more will our all-compassionate God treat those who never had the benefits that others had? "Do not judge and you will not be judged. Do not condemn, and you will not be condemned. Pardon, and you shall be pardoned" (Luke 6:37). I do not believe these less fortunate souls are held to the same standard as those of us who were fortunate enough to know Christ.

QUESTION #7

If, as is stated in the Bible, God knew us before we were born, and we accept the fact that God is involved in the birth of each of us, how does that affect the current controversy over abortion?

RESPONSE # 7

The quote you refer to is from the Prophet Jeremiah (1:4-5) "The word of the Lord came to me thus: Before I formed you in the womb I knew you, before you were born I dedicated you, a prophet to the nations I appointed you." In first grade we learned "Who made us? God made us to know Him, to love Him, and to serve Him..." God's involvement in the birth of each of us is to allow human beings to cooperate with Him in bringing other humans into the world. That is an awesome privilege to share with God in His power of creation. Sometimes I wonder if couples really understand that or do they just think that having a baby is just the result of sexual intercourse. Is God anywhere to be found in their picture of new life?

If the answer is no, God is not there, then it is rather easy to understand why the subject of abortion doesn't cause them any anguish. On the other hand, if God is in the picture, what effect does that have on the abortion issue?

Many religions have adopted the general principle that abortion is a form of murder if it is performed at or after the time that a soul enters the body of an embryo or fetus. Down through the ages, beliefs varied about when this "animation" happened. Some set a specific time of pregnancy as early as 40 days, others say 80 days, or as long as 116 days; and some say when the woman first feels the fetus move; while others say at conception.

Opinions vary on the abortion issue with most people generally falling into one of these four groups: 1.) those in favor of abortion at any time during pregnancy claiming that a woman, and only the woman, can decide what to do with her body; 2.) those in favor of abortion but only during the very early weeks of pregnancy (as outlined above) claiming that a fetus is not human life and argue that no one, including doctor or theologian, knows when the soul implants the body; 3.) those who, while opposed to abortion in general, support a woman's right to an abortion in the case of rape or incest. They use the principle of an "unjust assailant" for their position; and 4.) those who are totally opposed to all abortions regardless of the circumstances causing the pregnancy.

The decision over abortion has to be considered the most serious decision a woman or couple will most probably make in their lives because they are determining the fate of another life. There may be medical reasons to justify an abortion. But because abortion deals with the very sacred gift of life from God, we must always safeguard it as our most precious possession. Perhaps if we used a different word than "abortion" and called it "terminating life" we may focus more clearly on the reality and sharpen our moral sensibilities.

If a couple or any other person frustrates God's plan in creating another human being, they face very serious moral consequences for their decisions. Those decisions vary greatly and only the involved couple knows them to their full extent. If those decisions to abort are made lightly, frivolously, selfishly, or for convenience sake, the consequences certainly would seem to be much more serious. We know nothing as precious as life itself.

The Catholic Church has consistently taught that abortion at any stage of development is evil. Although Thomas Aquinas thought the soul did not come to the fetus ('ensoulment') until sometime after conception, he considered abortion gravely sinful even before conception. He taught that it was a grave sin against the natural law to kill the fetus at any stage, and a graver sin of homicide to do so after "ensoulment."

The decision to abort in no way eliminates God's loving care for the aborted baby.

QUESTION #8

Are all sins equal? Is it a greater sin to bring harm to others than to violate a commandment and thereby hurt our personal relationship with God?

RESPONSE #8

A sin is a sin is a sin is a sin! I don't see any difference between harming another or violating a commandment. Actually, harming another is a violation of a commandment also.

But for the sake of discussion: If a man slaps his wife in anger, does that offend her? If he has sex with another woman, does that offend her? They are both sins, and, of course, one is more serious than the other. The second part of your question seems to distinguish between sinning against others and sinning against God. I don't think we can separate the two. Remember Christ's response (Matthew 22:34-38) when the Pharisees tried to trip him up by asking "which commandment of the law is the greatest?" Jesus tells them "You shall love the Lord your God with your whole heart, with your whole soul, and with all your mind. This is the greatest and first commandment. The second is like it: You shall love your neighbor as yourself." Look very closely here at what Jesus says. The second commandment – love of neighbor - is JUST LIKE the first commandment. To me He is saying that there is no difference between the two. Really what He is saying is there is only ONE commandment – LOVE! You can't love God and not love your neighbor. It's like having a genuine coin which must have two sides, but it is still ONE coin. One more quote…"If anyone says, 'My love is fixed on God,' yet hates his brother/sister, he is a liar. One who has no love for the brother/sister He has seen cannot love the God he has not seen. The commandment we have from Him is this: whoever loves God must also love his brother/sister" (1 John 4:20-21). A sin against our neighbor is a sin against God and all sin harms our personal relationship with God and our neighbor.

QUESTION #9

When I open my heart to the Lord before taking communion and ask his forgiveness for the things that I've done and should not have done and those things that I should have done but failed to do, I usually pause at that point. Non performance is an area that is so easy to ignore. Is the sin of failing to do things that we know should have been done for God and others (acts of omission) as bad as acts of commission?

RESPONSE #9

Again, a sin is a sin is a sin! I think we should strive to get beyond measuring or trying to measure how much wrong or harm this or that action or non-action caused or what is the consequence of guilt associated with our commission or omission of actions. Let God be the judge of your actions and don't concentrate your attention so much on minutia. This kind of thinking can lead to scrupulosity (seeing sin where there is no sin; or seeing more serious defects where there are small defects) and it can create an unhealthy spiritual life and cause personality problems. Just try to live your life each day as pleasing as you can by being faithful to your state of life; love your family and friends; and try to maintain a happy and cheerful disposition, always ready to forgive, and ready to help others when you can. Focus your life on the positive aspects of being of service to those you love and meet.

QUESTION #10

Unless you're a sociopath, saint, or deeply grounded in psychology, you're likely on occasion to feel a sense of guilt for any one of many acts, thoughts, or deeds that were done or not done. How can a Christian minimize the feeling of guilt?

RESPONSE # 10

I think a Christian needs to follow many of the positive things I mentioned above in #9. We should "accentuate the positive" as the old song says. We should really develop a positive mental attitude about ourselves and everything related to us. That also means that we should also be what I call "realists". We need to see reality as it is and not as we wished it had been. The past is gone and we can't change it. We have only the present to work with. The future is yet to come. When we worry too much about our guilt and past, we are depriving Christ, ourselves, our loved ones, and others of the present. Remember the prophet Isaiah (1:18) "Though your sins be like scarlet, they may become white as snow."

QUESTION #11

Dealing with the death of a loved one is an issue that we all inevitably have to face. How should a Christian handle that event?

RESPONSE # 11

Read the beautiful story of the raising of Lazarus (John 11:1-44) and meditate on it! And then look for other beautiful passages in Scripture that speak about the after life John 16:4–33 speaks about Jesus' departure and the coming of the Holy Spirit. John 20:1–18 speaks of Christ's own resurrection. "In my Father's house there are many dwelling places" (John 14). "Eye has not seen, ear has not heard...what God has prepared for those who love Him"(1Corinthians 2:9). "The souls of the just are in the hands of the God... (Wisdom 3:1-3). "If we have died with Christ, we believe we shall also live with Him" (Romans 6:8-9). "What will separate us from the love of Christ?"(Romans 8:31-37). Realists, as I mentioned above have to face the fact that some day we will all die. That is a fact of life just like birth. No one is exempt, not our parents, nor uncles, aunts, brothers and sisters. So do not get overly anxious or sad when death knocks on your door. This doesn't mean that we should not grieve, nor that we may feel sad for our loss. But we as Christians have a lot to hope for. We do not see it as the end, but the beginning of all eternity with the Lord. "In the Lord's eye, one day is as a thousand years and a thousand years are as a day! (2 Peter 3:8).

Question #12

During Christmas and Easter we're reminded that we should put God at the center of our lives and subordinate all other worldly cares to following Christ. But, in the normal course of the events of each day it is extremely difficult to maintain that goal. The pressure for mere survival, advancement, pleasure, and dealing with temptations compete with what should be the number one priority. How can worldly issues be put into perspective with the need to have God as the center of our lives?

RESPONSE #12

In today's world it is very difficult to keep the spirit of any of our feast days centered on Christ. Christmas is now so commercialized that except for a few traditional Christian carols, no one would know that "Jesus is the reason!" Nativity scenes are rather uncommon. How many people will spend all kind of money on beautiful trees and fancy ornaments, plenty of lights outside, big dinners or group parties, but make no effort to put some kind of religious touch to these events. It doesn't cost much to have a little Christmas manger in your home and give it some prominence right near the tree. Light it up. Consider a manger on your lawn. Use other religious symbols around your home like cards with the nativity scene. Play some traditional carols as background music for your guests. Ask the youngsters in the family if they know who is in the manger and why, or ask if they know the words of the carols. It's hard to find religious Christmas cards, but look for them and send out only religious Christmas cards. Don't throw your tree out the day after Christmas. Christmas is a FULL SEASON. It is not just a day. Society has made Christmas and Easter like all the other "holidays" in the year – a purely commercial event to help boost sales of candies, clothes, and gifts. Refuse to be drawn into only that side of the holiday and keep these days as holy days putting an emphasis on the religious aspects at least for yourself and your family. And I didn't say much about Easter – the greatest feast of the entire Christian year. A foreshadow of our own resurrection. It is very difficult to be IN the world without being OF the world. That is the Christian's struggle!

QUESTION #13

When I ask myself how much of a Christian I really am, I usually come to the conclusion that I'm still learning, and that it will be more than a life long task. What constitutes being a Christian? Is it being born and raised in the Church and attending services and participating in the rituals? Or is it accepting Christ and trying to live by His example, teaching, and commandments – with all the failures and limitations that go with it? Or is it something else?

RESPONSE #13

Not being complacent is a good position in which to be. When you think you have already arrived, watch out for a great fall. All of us will still be learning even on our death beds, at least I hope so. What constitutes being a Christian? Going to church and rituals? I don't think so. Many people make religion their God, instead of making God their religion! Yes, what constitutes being a Christian is trying to live your life as Christ would have you live it. I don't think it is right to ask "what would Jesus do?" But rather, "what would Jesus want me to do?" There is a difference. Each of us is unique and we each have a unique role to play in doing God's will on earth. If I follow someone else, I might go down the wrong road. I have to follow the road He shows <u>me</u> and the way He shows me, yes, with all my limitations, failures, faults, gifts, talents, treasures, etc., etc, etc.

QUESTION #14

One of the conflicts that face most people is that of servant and master. As Christians we seek humility and service to God and our neighbors. But, our culture encourages us from childhood to succeed, to win, to be the best, and to accumulate as much as possible in both material wealth and prestige. How should we resolve this conflict, and is there a balance that allows us to do both?

RESPONSE #14

This has been a rather personal challenge for me in my own spiritual life. (Please excuse me while I get personal.) I lived for many years through the minor and major seminary and in religious life and priesthood with a vow of poverty. All during this time we were encouraged to practice detachment from material goods. We realized and understood that we had to use certain material things in order to live, but we were schooled in not seeking out the most comfortable or most expensive things, and always shied away from accumulating material possessions. We lived a rather simple life and our norm was to live as the middle class among those whom we were sent to serve. In both Puerto Rico and the Dominican Republic where I worked I saw real poverty up close among the people whom I served.

Yes, our culture encourages us to succeed, to win, to accumulate material wealth and prestige and honors, but we have to realize this is the "world" of which Christ spoke so often in contrast to the "kingdom of heaven" as he called it, especially in John's Gospel (John 15:18-19) e.g., "If you find that the world hates you, know it has hated Me before you. If you belonged to the world, it would love you as its own; the reason it hates you is that you do not belong to the world...".

Material goods, money, prestige and honors in themselves are not evil. (There is nothing that is evil "per se" (in itself) except sin.) It is our attachment, our desires to possess these things to the point where we are consumed in pursuing material things not for the promotion and extension of Christ's kingdom, but for our own benefit and that of our relatives, friends and acquaintances to advance our own agenda without a thought for the Kingdom of God. It is not wrong or sinful to seek to live in a large comfortable home, drive a nice car, have money in the bank, dress well and eat well, earn your way up the ladder of success at work, etc., etc.

This is what I learned about the struggle to balance wealth with the Gospel. <u>First</u>, realize that <u>everything</u> that you have is a gift of God. These are the blessings He has poured out upon you. Don't think of yourself as such a genius in having what you have as if it is all due to your ingenuity and talents. There are many smarter than you and more talented than you, who worked harder than you, but did not have all the good fortune and blessings that you had. St Paul tells us, "Name something you have that you have not received. If, then, you have received it, why are you boasting as if it were your own?" (1Corinthians 4:7). You should, therefore, be thankful to God for all these blessings. <u>Second</u>, don't squander these gifts and talents. Use your utmost efforts and abilities to develop and preserve these gifts and talents. <u>Third</u>, always share these gifts and talents with others! They weren't given to you for yourself, but for you to be Christ-like to others, to follow his example in loving others through your generosity.

The next question should be how do we reasonably share with others in today's world? The answer for each one of us will differ. No one knows your unique situation better than you do. For some it may be giving away money for a particular cause or foundation. For others it may be volunteering your time, talents, and treasure to a favorite charity. You may have a talent for working with the sick, aged, homeless, veterans, etc. Some volunteer to drive their handicapped neighbors to the doctors or shopping, or cooking for them. There are hundreds of ways we can share and give back to others. I am not advocating opening our doors and taking in the homeless or any other such risky responses in today's society. I have a friend who worked for many years for the disadvantaged and now retired, carries a dollar in his pocket every day to give to *the first needy person he sees. A dollar...not much, but, hey, that's $365.00 a year!*

It doesn't have to be 10% of your income or any such thing. The only important thing is that you follow the Lord's command to love one another...whatever that means in your particular circumstances. I'd like to suggest that you meditate on Christ's words in the Gospel of Matthew, Chapter 25:31–45, (it's about the last judgment) and then decide on your response.

QUESTION #15

It is said that faith can move mountains. As much as I seek to improve my understanding of God's word, the quest for unqualified faith is equally, if not more important to me. What is the measure of faith? At what point is it achieved? Is there a relationship between faith and our obedience to God's word?

RESPONSE #15

We have to define for ourselves what we mean by faith. The dictionary defines "faith" in the following ways, 1. A confident belief in the truth, value, or trustworthiness of a person, idea, or thing; 2. Belief that does not rest on logical proof or material evidence. 3. Loyalty to a person or thing. 4. Belief and trust in God; 5. Religious conviction. 6. A system of religious beliefs. 7. A set of principles or beliefs. In answering, I will presume the question means belief and trust in God, including religious conviction.

The quest for unqualified faith must be explained. For most of us humans, God does not communicate with us directly. We can address God directly through prayer day or night, but we can never be absolutely sure of God's response to us. There are those who have claimed that God spoke directly to them and gave them commands or instructions. But that does not happen ordinarily. The point is that it is difficult for us to know for certain God's will for us not only in every detail of our lives, but also in our major undertakings. We may and should seek counsel from more experienced people before making major decisions. Many people, besides praying for assistance, will seek the advice of parents, elders, clergy, or other professionals when trying to make major decisions in their lives. Yet none of these steps give us fool-proof certainty that we have made the right choice or that we are following God's will.

We can never lose sight of the fact that we are human beings and as such we are fallible and can never be absolutely sure that the decisions we make are the correct decisions - nor does God expect that of us. He is not a tyrant sitting on a throne with a black note book just waiting for us to fail and mark down every indiscretion and failing that we stumble over. No, our God is a merciful Father/ Mother who loves us dearly; loves us more than we love ourselves; more than the most loving of all human fathers/mothers possible. He is pulling for us all the time ready and willing not to notice our peccadilloes, faults and even our sins. We should remember again the words, "Come now, let us set things right, says the Lord: Though your sins be like scarlet, they may become white as snow; though they be crimson red, they may become white as wool" (Isaiah 1:18).

I would think that the measure of faith is to what degree we turn our lives over to God. Do we trust Him only in certain events in our lives, only on certain occasions? Do we trust Him only when things are going our way, when we are happy and successful? Or do we trust Him totally and unequivocally when we are in pain, hurting, suffering, down and out, without a job, misunderstood by our loved ones, unfairly denied our rights, hurting from betrayed friends, or the loss of a loved one? This total giving over of ourselves to God is a life-long process that only ends at our death. There definitely *is a relationship between faith and obedience to God's word. If one does not have faith in Christ, why would anyone obey God's word? It would make no sense. Obedience to God's word only makes sense if you believe in God. Recall Christ asking the apostles "Who do people say that the Son of Man is? They replied, 'Some say John the Baptizer, others Elijah, still others Jeremiah or one of the prophets.' 'And you,' He said to them, 'who do you say that I am?' 'You are the Messiah,' Simon Peter answered, 'the Son of the living God" (Matthew 16:13-16). Peter had total faith in Christ to the point of laying down his life for Him*

QUESTION #16

All too often people view God as something that is there to help their lives. Glorification, praise, and appreciation for all that the Almighty has made available, including our very lives, is overshadowed by prayers for help in time of need or desire. But, when the crisis is over or the problem solved God is often put back on the shelf. What can we draw upon to help our proper and humble relationship with God?

RESPONSE #16

God must be pretty accustomed to be called upon and then put back on the shelf until He is needed again. How many of us have been guilty of that from time to time? That is so human that only a divine being could stand for it. It reminds me of the atheist who during a terrible tornado was so full of fear that he screamed out, "Oh, God, help us!"

This way of dealing with God is like the first year college student who immediately calls home when he needs more money. When the crisis passes, he usually forgets to even call home. And mom and dad know all is well or they would get another phone call. But instead of focusing on the student, let's look at the parents. What is their reaction to this behavior? We aren't trying to excuse the student's selfish behavior, but focusing on how compassionate our God is with us.

How do we increase our awareness of God in our daily lives and not look to Him only in times of need? God is pure spirit and can not be seen so we have to develop ways to make ourselves aware of Him. We do this by adopting new habits of living. (Habits are formed by repeating the same action over and over.) So we need to find ways of reminding ourselves of God's continual presence. Some refer to this as "the sacrament of the present moment". Reading the Bible or spiritual reading books on how to develop various virtues and habits that can make us more aware of our human nature and tendencies, and developing the habit of daily prayer especially upon waking in the morning, before and after meals, or beginning a new task during the day, driving your car, starting your work for the day, or before retiring for the night. I remember a nun who taught me in the seventh grade and encouraged us to "Consecrate each day to God by turning this little golden key, 'My Jesus, all for Thee!" That was well over 60 years ago.

I am not suggesting that we turn ourselves into "religious fanatics" and wear long faces that seldom smile or are always quoting the Bible and sort of preaching to everyone we meet. No, we should follow Christ's advice about praying, "When you are praying, do not behave like the hypocrites who love to stand and pray in synagogues or on street corners in order to be noticed...Whenever you pray, go to your room, close your door, and pray to your Father in private..." (Matthew 6:5-6). Does this mean that we shouldn't pray in church which is a public place? No, this is telling us to be normal and human about our religious practices. Smile and be happy and pleasant with all whom you meet. Don't go around trying to convert everyone in sight and talk only about religion. That is a sure way of turning off people who otherwise may be willing to speak with you.

QUESTION #17

Worldly distractions and being overly focused upon ourselves often interfere with prayer and communication with God. While it's easy to say common prayers, it takes more concentration and thoughtfulness to honestly open your heart to God. Sometimes, I find it best to be quiet and listen for God to do the talking. Given the extreme importance of prayer, what can be done to facilitate communication with God?

RESPONSE #17

Some of the suggestions I made above about prayer apply to this response as well. Common prayers can become very routine almost to the point of being like a mantra devoid of any real meaning for the one saying or repeating it. Yet, there are many beautiful and meaningful common prayers that truly express our sentiments. We have to guard against these prayers becoming meaningless by saying them slowly and occasionally meditating on their content and meaning. Some prayers, like the prayer of St. Francis of Assisi, "Lord, Make Me an Instrument of Your Peace" can serve as an entire meditation and an examination of one's own way of life. We should find other written prayers and use them for our own prayer life if we can relate to them.

You mentioned "distractions and being overly focused upon ourselves" interfering with prayer. We should not be discouraged by these distractions because "prayer is the lifting of our hearts and mind to God" and each time we fight off the distraction, we are actually praying. It is our human nature that our minds wander and we drift off almost day dreaming during prayer. Remember God is not looking at results; He looks for our efforts. He can read our hearts and minds better than we can and He knows even before we ask what is best for us. "Your Father knows what you need before you ask him" (Matthew 6:8). Sometimes our seemingly feeble, distracted prayer may be more pleasing than one that fills us with the satisfaction of having "prayed well" in our opinion. "For my thoughts are not your thoughts, nor are your ways my ways, say the Lord. As high as the heavens are above the earth, so high are my ways above your ways and my thoughts above your thoughts" (Isaiah 55:8-9).

You mention that you find it best to be quiet and listen for God to do the talking. That is excellent prayer. Most folks think that they have to do all the talking and thus God can't get a word in edgewise. How are we going to know what He wants us to do if we don't listen to what He is telling us? This type of prayer is often referred to as quiet prayer where we just listen to God. Spiritual writers encourage us to seek this form of prayer and try to develop it. The busy hustle-bustle of modern day life makes this rather difficult for most people. So if that is your preference, do not abandon it. In fact, I encourage you to develop it further.

QUESTION #18

As evidenced by all my questions, Christianity is not easy to grasp, or to accept as the single focus of our lives. But when I think of what it means to me two words jump out – love and grace. Is that overly simplistic?

RESPONSE # 18

I would make it even more simplistic and just say LOVE. Perhaps I do not appreciate the full meaning that you give to "Grace". The dictionary says the theological meaning of "grace" is "divine love and protection bestowed freely upon mankind." So I see "grace" as God's love toward us.

Several years ago I worked with a man who tried to discover the single most important issue of whatever program on which we were working. He sought for the bare essentials. We would strip away everything we could until we got to the most basic element. It was a good way of helping us to keep a clear focus. We knew what to stress and what could be overlooked without detriment to the program.

I have applied this to Christianity and the Bible. What is the most essential teaching of everything that Christ taught? It would be difficult to read the New Testament without being struck by the overpowering references to love. Love of God and love of one another. Everything else depends on that! Love in the New Testament is like the hub of a wheel with every other story or event or saying passing through or connecting with LOVE. St. Augustine says it this way, "Love God and do as you please!" If we truly love God, we will only do good.

QUESTION #19

Each time that I say the Apostles Creed I reflect on my belief in miracles that Include Saints, the virgin birth, and all that go beyond human understanding. But, not all who claim to be Christians have that faith. How serious is it when they question one or more of the issues that are at the foundation of our religion?

RESPONSE #19

How serious is it when they question some of the issues of our religion? I think the best thing to remember in these situations is that not everyone is committed to his faith to the same degree. Growth in the spiritual life is somewhat similar to our natural growth. Not everyone enjoys a healthy body and not everyone cherishes his faith to the same degree that others do. Some folks are more serious about their health issues and that applies to the spiritual life as well.

I think we have to be very patient and understanding with those who may have a weak faith for whatever reason. Not that we are better than they, but because they may not have responded to God's grace in the same way, or perhaps they have not had the same opportunity to deepen their faith. If they came from an environment that did not assist them in deepening their faith, they may not be as convinced of their religion as others.

There are so many other reasons why they may question their relationship with God. I think the important thing is for those who truly believe to exercise extreme charity with such people, first, by not judging them, and secondly, letting them see the love and understanding that Christ would show them through our actions in dealing with them.

We should always remember Matthew 7:1-2. "If you want to avoid judgment, stop passing judgment. Your verdict on others will be the verdict passed on you."

QUESTION #20

Most of us who are blessed with children tend to refer to them as our children, when in fact it may well be better stated to say that they're God's children and that He graciously, and with confidence in our fidelity and obedience allows us to nurture, love, and help them to grow within His family. It's the greatest personal responsibility that we will ever have. Is it appropriate to view parenthood in that light?

RESPONSE #20

I have to say "yes" to both of your questions, Ernie. Yes, I believe procreating and raising children is the greatest personal responsibility that most of us will ever have. As mentioned above, in procreating, parents become co-creators with God in bringing new bodies and souls into existence to the honor and glory of God. And again yes, I believe it is appropriate to view parenthood in the light as you explain. However, I wouldn't quibble with saying that children are either God's children or ours because in a real sense both are correct. We are all God's children, yet children of our parents as well. I think that relationship expresses more than just a natural, human connection. I believe it helps us understand to some small degree who we really are to our God and what our relationship to Him is.

QUESTION #21

There are those who speak out against Christianity for what they see as hypocrisy. It's certainly true that few Christians manage to live up to the high standards of the Church. To varying degrees, people strive to comply with the commandments and obligations of Christianity, but most fall short. How should we view ourselves against such a charge, and what can we do to grow in the light of the Lord?

RESPONSE #21

About the year 313 AD the Emperor Constantine the Great issued a decree about the religious tolerance of Christianity. He made it fashionable to be a Christian and you can imagine how many people of all classes became "Christian". I don't know how many, but if you wanted to get ahead in society, you became a Christian. But how many really practiced that faith? The motives of many were very suspect and one can just imagine the amount of hypocrisy prevalent in those days. Of course, there were many sincere Christians, but I would not be surprised to learn that most became Christian for convenience sake alone.

Are there any Christians like that today? I would be naïve to say 'no'. But I will not point my finger at any one. I will not judge because it is not my place to do so. Christianity does not hold a monopoly on hypocrisy. Hypocrisy is doing very well these days in many other fields outside of religion. Just look at our politics, not only the politicians, but many of the voters as well. But religious hypocrites are probably the most glaring of hypocrites because most people expect more honesty and uprightness from church-going folks. And when some people see conduct or actions among Christians as unbefitting, or contrary to what they preach, they become critical. Is this right?

Judging others is easy and so commonplace. We must remember Christ's warning "If you want to avoid judgment, stop passing judgment. Your verdict on others will be the verdict passed on you. The measure with which you measure will be used to measure you" (Matthew 7: 1-2). So while there will always be those who judge others, our task as Christians is to try to live our lives according to our conscience. That's all God will judge us on. He is not going to judge us on what others think we should do, nor on what we actually do, but on how well we <u>try</u> to live as His followers. And I think this is what you are saying in your question that " to varying degrees, people strive to comply with the commandments and obligations of Christianity, but most fall short" It's the "trying" that really counts.

I once received some very good advice from a friend who told me, "Other people's opinion of who you are does not change who you really are!"

What can we do to grow in the light of the Lord? Considering the first part of your question, I think it would help if we do not get all upset and bothered by the criticism of others especially regarding the practice of our faith. Only you and God know your true motives and intentions and that is all that really counts. Of course, we are bound to avoid any conduct that would lead to scandal. "What terrible things will come on the world through scandal! It is inevitable that scandal should occur. Nonetheless, woe to that man through whom scandal comes!" (Matthew18:7). So we should continue to live our lives as best we can always using every new day and every new opportunity trying our best to become more Christ-like in all we do. This isn't easy and it does not mean becoming somber and spending the day in prayer and avoiding the joys and pleasures that God has given us with our spouse, family and friends. What I mean is do not wear your faith in God like a big outer garment that all people can see is "religion". Keep that garment invisible and let it dictate the unique and wonderful person that God has created for all the world to see.

QUESTION #22

It's often said that time is one thing that you never get back. Since we do not know how long we have on earth, it would seem that we should use each and every day for its own. And yet, our culture often has us working toward some future date to gain our rewards – graduation from college, promotion if we work hard for many years, raising children, retirement, maturing of investments, etc. How can we use every day that God has given us for the purpose that He put us on earth, and with the knowledge that our only real reward is eternal life through Christ?

RESPONSE #22

I think my response to #21 above sort of leads into this response. Being as faithful to our vocation in life as is humanly possible, whatever that may be, is the best way to use every day that God has given us to do His will. Being faithful to our vocation or state of life will be different for each person because each of us is different and unique. And some are given greater gifts than others and some are held to greater responsibilities than others. This should not surprise anyone. Just recall the laborers in the vineyard, Matthew 20:1-16. In this parable we see that the owner of the vineyard went out five different times and hired laborers, yet he paid them all the same The first laborers complained that they had worked longer and harder and should deserve more than the last ones hired. But you need to remember that those are man's rules; they are not God's! (Remember what I said earlier about dual thinking; it's "either/or"; "this or that". Not so with the Divine; it may be "both/and".)

We will all have a cross to carry (or may be many crosses), but we can't complain because only God knows why. The only rational way to face life (besides being the holiest way) is to joyfully accept whatever comes our way. That doesn't mean we have to run around with a big smile on our face because we have a terminal illness or a loved one has just passed away. No, it means not letting our crosses bog us down and make us feel like we have been chosen to suffer for the world. No matter our lot in life, if we try hard to keep our focus on God, He will provide us the grace to persevere.

QUESTION #23

It's not uncommon to hear people say that they believe in God, but do not consider themselves religious. Can you separate the two? More specifically, to be a Christian is there a requirement for learning, obedience, faith and association with the church?

RESPONSE #23

The dictionary defines "religion" as "a belief in and a reverence for a supernatural power recognized as the creator and governor of the universe." So those who distinguish between believing in God and not being religious are probably less than correct. I don't think you can actually separate the two. However, I have heard some people explain that although they believe in God, a Creator, or Supreme Being, they do not attend any religious services, or do not identify themselves as members of any established religion. Some of these folks will even admit to being spiritual, but not religious.

Are Christians "required" to learn, obey, live by faith, and associate with the church?

There are all kinds and degrees of Christians just as there are all kinds and degrees of Free Masons, Members of the Moose Club, or Lions or Elks, or any other society or organization. How serious are these participants about their organizations? Depending on their personal commitment and desire to participate, they will respond differently. Though being a Christian is much more serious than belonging to one of these social organizations, I think we would have to ask how serious are Christians about grace and their salvation.

My personal belief is that belonging to an organized church or not belonging isn't going to save or condemn anyone. I don't believe God will be asking us what Church we attended or to which religious sect we belonged on earth. All these institutions were established and organized by some men convinced that their way was the way to honor God on earth. I don't think that association with any established Church is a requisite for entering heaven, and I don't believe any such association is a requirement to be called a "Christian". A "Christian" is anyone who follows the teachings of Christ, no matter how well or poorly. There are Buddhists and Muslims who do not follow all the teachings of their founders either, but are still considered Buddhists and Muslims.

Remember the story of the rich young man asking Jesus what he had to do to be saved?

"Teacher, what good must I do to possess everlasting life? He answered, 'Why do you question me about what is good? There is one who is good. If you wish to enter into life, keep the commandments.' 'Which ones? he asked. Jesus replied, you shall not kill; you shall not commit adultery; you shall not steal; you shall not bear false witness; honor your father and mother; and love your neighbor as yourself. The young man said to him, I have kept all these; what do I need to do further? Jesus told him, if you seek perfection, go, sell your possessions, and give to the poor. You will then have treasure in heaven. Afterward, come back and follow me. Hearing these words, the young man went away sad, for his possessions were many" (Matthew 19:16-22). *Then Jesus tells His disciples about the danger of material goods and Christ's promise of granting everlasting life to "everyone who has given up home, brother or sister, father or mother, wife or children or property for My sake will receive many times as much and inherit everlasting life"* (Matthew 19:23-30).

What is interesting to me is that not once – nowhere – does Christ tell the young man to join the synagogue or mosque, or temple. Furthermore, I like to point out to Catholics, neither does He say anything about going to confession or the other sacraments, not even being baptized. We will be judged based on our love of God and our neighbor. Those who take this task seriously will try their best to love God and their neighbor with their whole mind, with their whole soul and with their whole body.

Now I'm not against Churches. They have their place – namely to help us learn how to know, love and serve God and our neighbor better

QUESTION #24

In reading the book of Mark I related to the all too common tendency of people to lack faith and trust in God when faced with a threatening situation. Contrary to the teachings of Christ, when the disciples were in the boat with Him and the sea was threatening He had to remind them that they should have faith in God and not fear the sea.

If, as close to the living Christ as the disciples were, they still lacked in faith and trust, it is not surprising that we too have a way to go to reach the teachings of the Lord and place our faith in God.

The terms, faith and trust seem to be very similar in their meaning. Is there a difference? What can we do as followers of Christ to increase our faith and lower our fear when faced with danger?

RESPONSE #24

You notice how I quickly run to the dictionary when you ask about the meaning of certain terms. That's just to be safe and make it easy for you to confirm my responses. You are right about faith and trust being very similar. Webster says that "faith" is (1) a confident belief in the truth, value, or trustworthiness of a person, idea, or thing. (2) Belief that does not rest on logical proof or material evidence. (3) Loyalty to a person or thing; allegiance; (4) Belief or trust in God. (5) Religious convictions. (6) A system of religious beliefs. (7) A set of principles or beliefs. "Trust" has many meanings too, but the one that seems closest to "faith" is "Confidence in the integrity, ability, character, and truth of a person or thing."

So, yes, these two words are rather similar, but there is a difference. Faith is having confidence in God or another person based on our past experience with God or the other person. We believe (have faith) in God because of His word and past promises and the knowledge we have gained from experience living our lives that He never fails. We have faith in our spouses and our children based on our past experience with them. I know that I can give my son a thousand dollars to deposit at the bank without any fear of losing the money.

Trust looks more to the future than faith does. We trust that we will be saved because of Christ's plan of salvation. We aren't saved yet, but we trust that if we live our lives as He wants, we will be saved. So when your spouse is undergoing a difficult operation, you have <u>faith</u> in the doctor because of his <u>past</u> experiences; but you <u>trust</u> in the success of your spouse's operation which is looking to the <u>future</u>.

The apostles asked Christ to increase their faith, and He answered: "If you had faith the size of a mustard seed, you could say to this sycamore, 'Be uprooted and transplanted into the sea' and it would obey you" (Luke 17:5-6). We can increase our faith by praying for a deeper faith every day. And each time we profess our faith in our daily lives either by words or deeds by trying to live as Christians, we increase our faith by deepening its roots and making us more aware of God.

It is only natural to fear when faced with danger. That fear can be very beneficial by making us take certain precautions to avoid the danger or at least minimize it. We will never totally eliminate our fears when faced with danger and tough decisions. That is a self-defense mechanism that keeps us alert, wise, and prepared.

But we must maintain a certain calmness through such times so not to become useless to ourselves and others. Some people can almost become irrational even with the slightest of dangers and can become their own worst enemy.

If we develop a spirit of daily prayer that keeps us in touch with the divine, it will serve us well in times of danger. We should develop the habit of praying during severe thunder and lightning storms; when starting out on long trips (even short one); when hearing the news of dangerous fires, earthquakes, tornadoes in other parts of the country or world.

QUESTION #25

God created the world. But today the world is divided among people who have different views of God. To what degree should Christians be tolerant of those who have a view of God that excludes Christ, and in some cases even show hostility toward Christians?

RESPONSE #25

All creation is the work of God and we have to respect His handiwork whether it appeals to us or not. We must remember that we do not know why Christ was revealed when He was revealed and to those to whom He was revealed. "He was in the world, and through Him the world was made, yet the world did not know who He was. To His own He came, yet His own did not accept Him. Any who did accept Him He empowered to become children of God" (John 1:10-12). To what degree should Christians be tolerant of those who have a view of God that excludes Christ? His entire message is one of forgiveness and love and not judging others. How can a true follower differ from this message? I believe that as Christians we have to be most tolerant of those who do not believe as we do. However, your question also speaks of hostility toward Christians. I don't think Christ is asking us to turn the other cheek in such circumstances of physical hostilities. We have an obligation to defend ourselves and our beliefs against unjust aggressors, and this should apply to acts of aggression that may be even less than bellicose. He warned, "They will harass you as they harassed Me" (John 15:20).

QUESTION #26

I personally do not advocate or encourage homosexuality, and I oppose same sex marriage. But, I also don't condemn all homosexuals. We know without question that gender identity is often a physical factor that is pre-determined before birth. On the other hand, and for obvious reasons, it seems to be clear that God intends that in the joining together of two people that they be male and female. While someone who practices homosexuality may elect to do so, many people inherit the proclivity at birth. Since God creates us, is it proper to question His actions? What is said in the Bible that warrants such a strong reaction to homosexuality by many people? How should we as Christians view this issue?

RESPONSE #26

Is it proper to question God's actions about creation? No, I don't think it is. There are thousands of "out-of-the-ordinary" births in the world, and I am not referring only to physical differences. We should never try to second guess God about His creation or anything else that He does since He is our Creator. He owes us nothing.

You ask what the Bible says regarding homosexuality. The Old Testament rejects homosexual behavior. You can find an account of two angels in disguise who go to the city of Sodom where Lot shelters them. Some men from Sodom insist that Lot give the disguised angels to men in Sodom for homosexual intercourse. Lot resists and the men of Sodom are made blind by the angels. The town is destroyed by fire "because the outcry against its people has become great before the Lord" (Gen.19:13). Lot and his household escape

In Jude 7 we find that Sodom and Gomorrah "acted immorally and indulged in unnatural lust." Ezekiel says that Sodom committed "abominable things" (Ezek. 16:50), which could refer to homosexual and heterosexual acts of sin. Lot even offered his two virgin daughters in place of his guests, but the men of Sodom rejected the offer, preferring homosexual sex over heterosexual sex (Gen. 19:8–9).

Leviticus also condemns homosexuality: "You shall not lie with a male as with a woman; it is an abomination. . . . If a man lies with a male as with a woman, both of them have committed an abomination; they shall be put to death, their blood is upon them" (Lev. 18:22, 20:13).

In the New Testament Paul says, "For this reason God gave them up to dishonorable passions. Their women exchanged natural relations for unnatural, and the men likewise gave up natural relations with women and were consumed with passion for one another, men committing shameless acts with men and receiving in their own persons the due penalty for their error. And since they did not see fit to acknowledge God, God gave them up to a base mind and to improper conduct. . . . Though they know God's decree that those who do such things deserve to die, they not only do them but approve those who practice them" (Rom. 1:26–28, 32).

And Paul also speaks out against homosexual behavior this way "Do you not know that the wicked will not inherit the kingdom of

God? Do not be deceived: Neither the sexually immoral nor idolaters nor adulterers nor male prostitutes nor homosexual offenders nor thieves nor the greedy nor drunkards nor slanderers nor swindlers will inherit the kingdom of God" (1 Cor. 6:9–10).

How should we as Christians view this issue? I think it is clear from Scripture that homosexuality is a sin. There is very little room, if any, to disagree with that.

Elsewhere in these questions and responses we speak of hating the sin, but not the sinner. And I think this applies here as well. We must remember first, not to judge; and second, to distinguish between homosexuals and homosexuality.

I am not educated enough in medicine or psychology to completely understand why a person is homosexual. I've mentioned elsewhere that we are finite and as such we are limited in our understanding of many things in God's creation. For me, this is one of them. From my limited experience in conversing with homosexuals, I can not imagine why anyone would arbitrarily choose that life style. But I am aware that many believe that for some, it is a deliberate choice.

While I am opposed to same sex marriage (homosexuality) morally because, like you, I believe that marriage is between a man and a woman, I support the right of homosexuals to partake of the same rights as heterosexual partners for the purposes of tax breaks and inheritance, and other benefits, etc.

Now I would not at all be surprised if you would think that I am being at least somewhat inconsistent here because you may see my position as contradictory. You may argue that by granting homosexuals the same privileges as those of heterosexuals I would be condoning homosexuality itself. First, I would respond by saying that I can't conceive of preventing one class of citizens from enjoying *a benefit based solely on sexual orientation and especially when I am not in their shoes. But more importantly, to deny homosexuals the same rights that others enjoy appears to me to be grossly unfair, unjust, and unconstitutional. (Remember, I believe in the separation of church and state and that the state's role covers the temporal order and not the moral order.) By providing the same benefits (a purely temporal matter) to homosexuals that heterosexuals enjoy, the question of the possibility that this action could be seen as condoning homosexuality (a moral issue) has absolutely nothing to do with granting homosexuals equality. It is not the state's primary responsibility to ensure proper morals among its people; only to provide justice and equality and protection under due process of the law. I have no objections to the Church or anyone else trying to influence the state to prevent laws that they deem as immoral. I am fully aware that if you do not share my view of separation of church and state, then you will not agree with my position either.*

QUESTION #27

While I've repeated it many times over the years, when I recently sang the Agnus Dei before communion it brought forth a new meaning with the words, "Jesus, Lamb of God; you take away the sin of the world:---." In that statement the blessing of Christ doesn't seem to be limited to only those who recognize Him as their personal savior, but rather all people in the world. Is the intended implication that we're all God's children, and He's there for whoever listens or reaches out? What should I take away from the meaning of the AGNUS DEI?

RESPONSE #27

Your question demonstrates to me my very strong and deep-seated belief that the "...Spirit begets spirit. Do not be surprised that I tell you,

you must all be begotten from above. The wind blows where it will. You hear the sound it makes but you do not know where it comes from, or where it goes" (John 3:6-8). As responsible and discerning people God does speak to us as you demonstrate in this question. Christ did not give His body to eat to just the healthy ones. He is the master physician who came to heal us all, not just those who go to church.

You will recall the Passover ritual described in great detail in Exodus 12. Moses tells the people to procure a lamb that is a year old male and without blemish. They are to slaughter the lamb during the evening twilight and apply some of its blood to the two doorposts and lintel of every house in which they partake of the lamb. They are to eat the lamb that night with unleavened bread and bitter herbs. Then he tells them how to eat it because it is the "Passover of the Lord". The "Passover" is the angel passing over the Israelites and sparing them from death to the first-born of the home.

Also in the Old Testament you will find that they worshipped God by sacrificing a lamb over which the priest or leader would "lay his hand on the head of the holocaust, so that it may be acceptable to make atonement for him" (Leviticus 1:4). This symbol of laying hands on the lamb also signified that the priest in the name of the community was laying all the community's sins and transgressions on the lamb. This was their way of seeking forgiveness from God. And today in our liturgies we invoke the name of Jesus by calling Him the "Lamb of God who takes away the sin of the world". Here is how a short article in the Wikipedia explains it, "A sacrificial lamb is a <u>metaphorical</u> reference to a person or animal <u>sacrificed</u> (killed or discounted in some way) for the common good. The term is derived from the traditions of <u>Abrahamic religion</u> where a <u>lamb</u> is a highly valued possession, but is offered to <u>God</u> as a sacrifice to obtain the more highly valued favour of God. This is a direct reference to <u>Jesus Christ</u> who, in death, is traditionally considered to have played the role of a sacrificial lamb."

PART TWO

OUR RELATIONSHIP WITH EACH OTHER

OUR RELATIONSHIP WITH EACH OTHER

Many who question the existence of God claim that virtue, kindness, compassion, and justice are not the exclusive purview of religion, but rather qualities that are inherent in mankind. Not surprisingly, they can point to people and incidents of the past to support the notion that there indeed have been some favorable contributions to mankind that were motivated by reasons other than religion. Further bolstering their argument, they can point to the historic record of deeds done in the name of religion that were the antithesis of Christian values – certainly the Inquisition and numerous wars.

It's true that man left to his own design is less than perfect. There are many examples that show that people who have professed to be Christian, or devout members of another religious faith, have committed atrocities that then become attributable to the religious faith of the man or men. But, does that warrant a conclusion that there is no difference in the motivation and decisions between those who are without a faith in God and those who look to a higher authority for guidance? Or is it merely evidence that man is not perfect, consistent, or always honest?

Another measure of looking at man's relationship with man is to compare the condition of human life prior to the presence of Christ on earth against the current condition 2000 plus years later. Clearly, not all advancements in humanity can be attributed to Christianity. But, when you look around the world and see the acts of compassion done in the name of Christ, it would be hard to deny that the Christian movement has had a very significant effect on the value placed on human life.

Christianity as practiced by mortal men is certainly less than perfect, but there is an effort to grow and improve. As the influence of the Church moves throughout the world there's reason to be optimistic that the lessons from our Christian/Judaic heritage will help bring about improved conditions in human relations.

Two thousand years ago Christ stood alone with only twelve followers in preaching the manner in which God's children should act toward their brothers and sisters. Today His message reaches out to billions of people in every corner of the earth.

In truth, people without a moral compass that points to God will generally move toward the direction of what is in their personal best interest. But, given faith in God, they will move beyond their personal interest and live their lives in the knowledge that they are His children and committed to his commandments – among which is love thy neighbor as thy self.

Frank, please feel free to add any comments.

Ernie, I would just observe that there are only eight questions in this section and if anyone were to judge the importance of the four sections by the number of questions posed, this section would be the least important. And yet, just the opposite is the truth! If you look closely at the other three sections, you will see that almost all the questions in some way or other revolve around our relationship with each other.

We are social beings and do not and cannot survive in a vacuum or live alone on an island. Our entire lives are intertwined with one another. It is only the sociopath, the sick among us, who want to live alone. Even if we live alone by circumstances, having the minimum number of contacts possible, we still depend on one another in so many ways. The interplay among us is just phenomenal. At the end of a normal day, just think of how many people you interacted with that day. Many of them, most of them, were not by your own choice, were they? Yet, they were and are a part of your life.

For the true Christian seeking a deeper spiritual life of union with God, he will ask some questions at the end of the day. How did I treat these people who came into my life? Mind you, it doesn't matter how they came into your life. What was my attitude toward them? Could I have done something to improve their lives? Here is some advice from St. Paul! "Look on the needs of the saints as your own; be generous in offering hospitality. Bless your persecutors; bless and do not curse them. Rejoice with those who rejoice, weep with those who weep. Have the same attitude toward all. Put away ambitious thoughts and associate with those who are lowly. Do not be wise in your own estimation. Never repay injury with injury. See that your conduct is honorable in the eyes of all. If possible live peaceably with everyone" (Romans 12:13-18). And again, "All of you who have been baptized in Christ have clothed yourselves with Him. There does not exist among you Jew or Greek, slave or freeman, male or female. All are one in Christ Jesus" (Galatians 3:27-28). You see, real, authentic Christianity isn't for the faint of heart. It's a daily encounter and isn't easy. Remember, "Whoever wishes to be My follower must deny his very self, take up his cross each day, and follow in My steps" (Luke 9:23) and (Mark 8:34).

Part Two

Our Relationship with Each Other

Questions

&

Responses

QUESTION #1

In the brief period of our life-time we have seen an almost revolutionary change in culture and values. Among those changes is the traditional family.

The role of parents has changed. In many families the father is no longer the primary source of financial support, or even the head of the family. All too often, the mother is no longer the source of nurture for the children. Divorce, once discouraged, is now commonplace. One-parent families have also risen at an alarming rate. With the trend toward "political correctness", such issues are rarely discussed. How, if at all, does this change in culture affect society from a spiritual or Christian perspective?

RESPONSE #1

I don't think anyone fifty years or older will deny that our world has changed drastically in many ways and that our spiritual values and Christian perspective has changed almost as drastically. When my parents who died in 1969 and 1974 raised their family, they knew the blueprint for raising a family...just follow what their parents did in raising their family. But when my sisters and brothers had their families (especially the younger ones) they found that the blueprint that my parents used was now broken and pretty much discarded. Society had changed.

If I may digress, I would say that the one biggest cause for the drastic change in society from that of our parents was the invention of television. Prior to TV, one had to go to a theatre of some sort to find visual entertainment; now we had it right in our living room and in a short time it was there during all the waking hours and then 24/7. I remember hearing that when they first started to show movies on TV that in one year, TV had shown 25 years worth of movies. When we were kids our parents wouldn't let us see a movie at the local movie house unless it had received a rating that was proper for children. The ratings were published in the Legion of Decency listing. Heaven help us if we went to the movies and our parents found out it was not approved for children. With TV right in your living room, what happened to the Legion of Decency ratings?

This is just one small example of how things began to change our spiritual or Christian values. All the other aspects you mention contributed to a slow, but sure change in how we viewed and lived our values. Consumerism and our voracious appetites to accumulate material goods contributed greatly to challenging and lessening our spiritual values.

We have to remember that those values that we knew when we were growing up came from a long line of family traditions that were almost considered sacred. We had role models in our older sisters and brothers and they taught us our lessons without our realizing it. Respect toward parents and elders, family bonds with grandparents, uncles, aunts, and cousins, discipline in the home, parents' support of teachers, the position of the Church in family life, a sense of honesty with family and neighbors, the value of a nickel, etc., etc. All of these elements in our society taught us a system of proven values on which we could rely.

Then an erosion of the same left a drastic affect on all of us. We changed, but we changed so quickly that there never was time to adjust properly. And probably the saddest and most devastating change of all was the loss of the spiritual and Christian values. And we are still trying to recover from it all to this day.

Question #2

Being a Christian isn't easy. Among the challenges is the commandment that we love our neighbor and help those in need and less fortunate. When we're having a good day, most Christians try to comply. But, we're not always having a good day, and there are times when we're not as willing to extend ourselves to others, particularly those with whom we disagree or are seen in an adversarial way. How can we overcome that threshold of selfishness and take on the cares and needs of others?

RESPONSE #2

You hit upon an up-hill battle that all of us face daily. It's hard to be on the top of your game every day, all day. We are just too human to excel at every moment of our lives no matter how good our intentions are. But don't become discouraged by any of that. God does not expect us to be perfect; to hit a home-run every time we bat; dance a perfect dance each time we hear a beautiful waltz; or make a perfect meal every day of the week. It is not the result that he looks for, it is our effort. And some days our efforts may not be 100%, but then again, he understands that too.

You ask how can we overcome that threshold of selfishness. I believe it was St Francis Xavier who said that "we are so full of self, that it dies 15 minutes after we do." The struggle against selfishness is a life-long one. Again, I don't think that the Lord wants us to get all up tight and anxious about our selfishness. He wants us to be aware of it and often to think about our selfishness and continually chip away at it like a sculptor chipping away on a block of marble to create a beautiful statue. Just remember, the statue may take years to take form and may never be finished. Patience!

His command is to love one another as we love ourselves. That is very important and perhaps a good place to begin...loving ourselves. The Greeks had a saying, "know yourself." That is the beginning of knowledge. Someone once said, "Knowing others is intelligence; knowing yourself is true wisdom. Mastering others is strength; mastering yourself is true power." We may know ourselves, but do we really love ourselves? We have to look in the mirror and see ourselves with all our faults and failings, but realize that we are much, much more than that.

In my comments at the beginning of this Part Two, I mentioned how we should take on the cares and needs of others. St. James (1:27) gives us this advice, "Looking after orphans and widows in their distress and keeping oneself unspotted by the world make for pure worship without stain before our God and Father."

Many of us probably look around and see the terrible need there is to help others, especially at this time when so many are without work and means of support. All these people certainly can be and should be objects of our charity and giving.

All of us probably receive far more solicitations in the mail for financial help than we can reasonably handle, especially for those on a fixed income like so many people today. It just becomes impossible to give to everyone. I find it useful to pick a few of my favorite charities based on causes that have a personal connection to illnesses that family members have experienced. Then send a yearly donation to several of them.

In addition some may have their own family members who are in financial need. And I believe that "charity begins at home." Helping our own needy family members certainly falls under the same cloak of charity.

QUESTION #3

It's often said that actions speak louder than words. I never cease to be impressed when I see small acts of kindness, particularly among strangers. I have heard that the idea has reached some public attention with the term, "Pay it Forward." The concept, while simple, is not one that would come naturally to most people. But, among thinking and caring people it seems to be catching on. It basically takes the form that when you get the opportunity to show a bit of kindness to someone and their response is both appreciative and a little surprised, you can merely say, "Pass it on". Hopefully, in the not too distant future they'll reciprocate in an act of kindness to someone else, and in time the world will be a better place. While it may not be done in the name of Christ, it seems to capture His teachings. How do you view such an effort?

RESPONSE #3

I fully support the idea of "Pay it Forward", "Move it forward", "Pass it on" or whatever you may want to call it. There is a wonderful T.V. commercial by some insurance company that shows about 8 or 9 different scenes of people helping others. A man picking up a toy for a lady with a little baby; a fellow helping someone who has just fallen in the rain; a worker who pushes her fellow worker out of the way of some falling boxes, etc. It could be a commercial for any Christian religion because it's all about helping others.

We used to live next to a very kind older Christian neighbor who was always ready and willing to help us out with different projects, like tuning up my car, putting in an attic fan, or showing me how to replace the wax ring around a toilet bowl. He was so generous with his time. One day as he was doing something for me, I said, "Jim, I'm embarrassed that you are always so ready and willing to help me and I can't do anything for you." He cut me off and said, "Frank, don't worry about it. Today is my turn; tomorrow it will be yours." Boy, was Jim right!

The next day I went to work and, as usual, drove a commuter van as my method of transportation. Shortly after I arrived at work, a fellow worker approached me and said, "Frank, did you drive your van today? I told her I had. Then she told me that someone broke her car window during the night and asked if I could go with her to drop the car off at the repair shop. Our boss gave us permission and off we went. As soon as Sharon had dropped off the car and got into my van, she said, "Frank, you can't imagine how much I appreciate this. I am so..." I cut her off and told her about my neighbor Jim... "Sharon" I said, "today it is my turn, tomorrow it's yours!"

I am sure you have had many opportunities while driving to give another driver the courtesy of getting in front of you at a merge or wherever. Did you ever happen to stay behind that person and watch them do the same thing? It's usually contagious.

And you know what? It may not be done explicitly in the name of Christ, but the good act helps spread a sense of gratitude and good will among others and I honestly believe that that comes from God even without anyone realizing it. How many times have you experienced an act of kindness, or had someone do you an unexpected favor, or done something to aid another person on the spur of a moment without any forethought? Those to me are done by and through the interactions of our guardian angels.

Question #4

When I meet people who are overly self-righteous, highly critical of others and with little concern for the plight of the less fortunate, I find it hard to smile. In my view, they may feel that they have faith and hope, but they forgot the need for love. On the other hand, when you see someone who quietly lives the life of a practicing Christian you can usually tell it by the joy that he/she radiates. Your thoughts?

RESPONSE #4

Everything happens for a purpose. I did not really want to go to the Dominican Republic (DR) when my superiors transferred me there. I loved Puerto Rico and the people and my priestly work. But I went to the DR without complaining. And today I look back on that experience as probably the best thing that ever happened to me; not only because I eventually married a Dominican lady, but because of the experiences that I would never have had otherwise. Recently, another married priest friend who spent four years in the DR told me that those years changed him as no other years had done.

At the time we served there, the DR was close to being a third-world country. And life was about as simple as it gets. We saw people struggling to live in a community with the bare necessities of life. The people were not sophisticated, snobbish, or pretentious. They didn't pretend to be other than what they were and you could see. I never remember ever trying to convert any of them to our religion if they were of another one. Theirs was a deep respect for priests and their friendliness and kindness knew no bounds. And much of our work outside of the religious services was to assist the people with the necessities of life, food, clothing, medicine and work projects.

But all this experience taught me to look at life in a completely different way than if I had never left the U.S.A. To this day, more than 40 years later, I realize that I have been formed in a way that made me different than who I would have been without that experience. I know that I see many problems and issues discussed in the U.S.A. differently than many Americans simply because I was exposed to a different perspective.

It's like you say, it is difficult to try and fathom how people in our society can so easily and almost carelessly brush aside the needy no matter who they may be, including illegal immigrants. Of course, I am not defending those who refuse to work or get a cure for addictions that render them incapable of supporting themselves. Some Christians criticized us for being "social workers" among the people and not priests. I used to respond that Pope Pius XII said something to this effect, "If you talk to a hungry person about God, his stomach is talking louder than you are; give him something to eat first." That sounds like St. James (2:15-17) "If a brother or sister has nothing to wear and no food for the day, and you say to them, 'Good-bye and good luck. Keep warm and well fed,' but do not meet their bodily needs, what good is that?"

QUESTION #5

Seeking revenge is an all too often characteristic of humans. As Christians we learn about the importance of forgiveness, loving those who have wronged us and helping to bring about reconciliation. Unfortunately, that knowledge often fails in favor of the tendency to get even with our adversaries. How should we react when hurt, abused, or victimized?

RESPONSE #5

We need only read the passion of Christ in any of the four gospels to see how Christ reacted to false accusations. They betrayed Him, told lies about Him, invented stories, ridiculed Him, laughed at Him, spat upon Him, beat Him with whips, slapped Him, crowned Him with thorns, and finally crucified Him. And the amazing thing is that with a whisper He could have done away with all of them...but He did not. He turned the other cheek.

When we are hurt or abused or offended we should think of Christ and not become inordinately upset and try immediately to defend ourselves and confront our abusers. We should try to acquire some of Christ's humility and swallow some of the criticism as atonement for our own sins and failings. And we should remember Christ hanging on the cross and praying for His enemies...yes, praying for them..."Father, forgive them; they do not know what they are doing" (Luke 23: 34).

And what about the prayer that Christ Himself taught us? "Father, forgive us our sins as we too forgive all who do us wrong...(Luke 11: 4). Can we truly say this with meaning if we do not forgive everyone who has offended us? Can we hold a grudge against anyone and dare to pray this prayer, regardless of what they may have done to us? If we hold a grudge and say this prayer, we are in effect telling God NOT to forgive us because we haven't forgiven either.

You know a lot of people seek revenge after they have been hurt or offended. They think that "they will get even". Have you ever tried to get even? I tried it. I found out that "getting even" doesn't really get me even. It makes me feel sort of stupid, dumb, and embarrassed. I don't really like myself when I try to get even. Yeah, it makes me very "uneven".

Christianity is all about LOVE...of God and neighbor...and love without FORGIVENESS is a mockery.

Question #6

Most Christians and atheists claim to have a concern for their fellow man and to be compassionate. If that's a reality, is there any difference between them as to their values and how they conduct their lives? A quick glance might lead one to say no and that it would be difficult to tell which person showing compassion is a Christian and which is an atheist. But, if you would engage each in discussion as to their reasons for showing concern about their fellow man I believe that the issues of love, as taught by Christ, would help differentiate them. In the mean-time, let's hope that until the atheists find Christ that they at least continue to be considerate and kind. Do you see any significance in the manner that each approaches life?

RESPONSE #6

I am not sure I know any declared atheists, though I certainly feel that I have met many people who have left me wondering if they really believe there is a God. In the Epistle of Titus, (1:16) we read, "They claim to 'know God,' but by their actions they deny that He exists..." I am not referring to the generous atheists you speak about.

The difference between atheists and Christians, I would hope, is that the Christians are motivated in their concerns for others because they know that we are all brothers and sisters of the same Father. "Have we not all the one Father? Has not the one God created us? Why then do we break faith with each other violating the covenant of our fathers? (Malachi 2:10). There are some very generous philanthropists who are motivated to share large sums of their fortunes with others apparently for no spiritual motive. I wonder if that is really true or are they afraid to admit they do indeed follow Christ? I have no idea, but I find it very difficult to understand how someone would expend themselves toward others so much without some kind of compassion in their hearts, and I would think that is extremely close to what Christ addressed. I wonder, in the end, does it matter what the atheists' real motive was for giving, as long as they felt it their duty to share? How could the good Lord find fault with some of the outstanding contributions that many atheists have made? Could it be that they give perhaps without the "purest" of motives, but they do have some motive other than pure self love?

QUESTION #7

Psychology and psychiatry, as off-springs of philosophy with touches of science, have ushered in a new and more liberal view of how we see people with non-conforming attributes.

It's recognized that God, in His ultimate wisdom, does not create all people exactly the same. While we differ in our talents, abilities, and characteristics we all have in common that we are His children and have a soul.

As a general rule the acceptance of all types of behavior is not totally agreed upon. The law allows for consideration of some extreme human problems, but for the most part we still expect conformity to the norm, and those who for whatever reason are unable to meet that standard often suffer the criticism of society. While the list of non-conformist acts is long and broad, the most common are focused on sexual behavior and life style.

To what extent should Christians be tolerant of people who seem unable or unwilling to conform?

RESPONSE #7

I think that Christians have to be extremely tolerant of people who seem unable or unwilling to conform to what we call the "norm". (Someone once told me that what we call the "norm" is because that is what the majority of people favor or do, but that does not necessarily constitute it being the truth or the correct way to act.) So could the majority be wrong?

Your question takes me back once more to what I have mentioned about "loving our neighbor". We can not be arrogant and set ourselves up as "the authority" on virtue, life style or behavior any more than we can determine to which political party everyone should belong, or what is the best book to read on the Bible, or to which Church everyone should belong. I know you will say that my examples are not in the same category as "virtue, life-style and behavior" but to those who have not accepted Christ, or who practice no religion, it probably would make no difference.

Again, look at Christ's life. He was surrounded by all kinds of people who hated Him, yet He treated them all with kindness, sometimes sternness, but always with love. You remember the quote, "love the sinner, but hate the sin." That sounds nice, but that is probably difficult for most human beings especially if someone does something against us personally or our loved ones. God can love the sinner and hate the sin, but we probably would struggle with that. God's love is endless, human love is limited.

As human beings, we are imperfect and, therefore we cannot love or hate perfectly. But God can love and hate perfectly, because He is God. God can hate without any evil or malicious intent. So, since God can not sin, He can hate the sin and the sinner in a justifiable way while still being able to forgive the sinner when He repents.

QUESTION #8

Is mankind inherently good and without the need for the acknowledgment and acceptance of God? There seems to be an ever increasing debate between those who believe that religion in any form should be excluded from government or any public element of society, and that religion should be a private matter. The core issues currently in dispute include whether the common values of compassion, honesty, freedom, and justice are virtues that are not necessarily founded in religion, but rather are common to all people, even atheists. In short, do we need to acknowledge religion as the source of determining the values of society?

RESPONSE #8

This is a tough question. I can only give a qualified "yes" to this question. I think the vast majority of mankind in general is inherently good, but with a very strong tendency toward evil because of our fallen nature, and because of the constant bombardment from the devil. We can overcome some of these attacks, not by ourselves, but with the acceptance and acknowledgement of God's grace. God's grace is absolutely necessary in this struggle because we are up against a very powerful foe that we must recognize as a spiritual being whose powers and influence are far superior to ours. We can not battle the supernatural with the natural. That is why God's intervention on our behalf is so vitally important. We would be foolish to think that while the devil could tempt Jesus Christ (Luke 4:1-13); we ourselves can not be tempted.

I think we need to keep religion and government separate. The purpose of religion is, first, to make human beings aware of the Almighty and then assist human beings in developing a relationship with God. The purpose of government is to establish, and administer laws for the good of society – the common good. The realm of religion is totally spiritual, while that of the government is the material world. They are mutually exclusive.

I believe our Constitution states it correctly when it says that the government should not have any approved religion. Our Constitution does not forbid or prohibit any of us, including the government, from outward expressions of our belief in God. We are a country founded on the belief of a Creator. So if this is our very foundation, I think it absolutely foolish for anyone to insist that any public outward display or expression of religion should be outlawed.

You mention that the core issues currently in dispute include whether the common values of compassion, honesty, freedom, and justice are virtues that are not necessarily founded in religion, but rather are common to all people, even atheists. In short, do we need to acknowledge religion as the source of determining the values of society?

I think that if we address many values in our society, but especially those that you mention, the degree to which they are embraced and practiced without the acknowledgement of religion is very shallow, inconsistent, and superficial for most people concerned.

There is no doubt that there are many people who possess those virtues that you mention and who have no religious affiliations. They are just good folks who believe in being compassionate, fair, honest, and just. But the great majority of people are not that way. There is just too much selfishness in the world to expect otherwise. For example: if ten people found a wallet with $300.00 dollars in it, do you think all ten would try to return it to the owner? Now I'm not saying that if the ten people belonged to an established religion, that all ten would return it. The temptation is there for everyone, but religion, hopefully, should awaken a deeper sense of honesty.

So even if we concede that human beings are inherently good, that does not obviate the need for religion to increase their capacity to develop a deeper sense of obligation respect and honor toward one another.

I also want to add that I do not totally agree that all those virtues that you mention above are common to all people, even atheists. Even today we see leaders and others in some countries who do not exhibit all of these virtues. The gross and inhumane treatment by some of these people exemplifies only too well that "all" people are not inherently good. Some seem almost to portray that they are inherently evil.

Often times many people exhibit what on the surface may look like one or the other of the virtues you mentioned above, but if we look closely we will find that while their action or conduct seemed to be a virtue, it was in effect done for some other motive, perhaps, selfishness, embarrassment, pressure, or some other reason other than plain, simple kindness, compassion, or charity.

I am reminded of Christ telling the apostles "if one of you knows someone who comes to him in the middle of the night and says to him, 'Friend, lend me three loaves, for a friend of mine has come in from a journey and I have nothing to offer him'; and he from inside should reply, 'Leave me alone. The door is shut now and my children and I are in bed. I cannot get up to look after your needs' – I tell you, even though he does not get up and take care of the man because of friendship, he will do so because of his persistence, and give him as much as he needs"(Luke 11:5-8). Christ knew our human nature very well. He also knew that we could be embarrassed or pressured into doing the right action for the wrong motive.

Part Three

The Bible

THE BIBLE

It's been called the most important book in the world, and for good reason. Among other things it's the authoritative record and foundation for the faith of Christians. In addition, it provides the guidelines, rules, and commandments for a large part of the world's culture, values, and judicial systems. But, as with all complex and far reaching subjects, it is not easy to properly comprehend.

Having been written by a series of people from different cultures and languages over a long period of time, and then translated many times to enable people all over the world access to the message, without a background in theology the Bible is a challenge for the average person to read. Understandably there are differences in opinion on the meaning and emphasis, some of which have risen to the point of bringing forth splits in Churches and varying views on issues of faith. But, even allowing for all those challenges, the Bible remains the rock upon which billions of people live their lives.

What follows in the way of questions and responses is not intended to be a complete list of all the issues that warrant thoughtful discussion. But, hopefully those who seek to better understand the world's greatest document will find it a useful step in their pursuit to know God.

Frank, I'm sure that you want to make some introductory comments on this section.

Yes, I do, Ernie, mainly because of the prominence that the Bible holds among Christians, and, secondly, to point out some of the challenges the reader faces when reading this sacred book.

In your preface you mentioned that some folks have not progressed theologically beyond what they learned when they were children. I can say "amen" to that a thousand times over! And just as true as that is, so is it true that Biblical scholars have not stood still in their quest to understand the Bible more thoroughly. As you know, studies continue today into the times and life of Christ and the meaning of words and figures of speech used then. The results are that we know a lot more today about those times than we used to and if we do not consider these new discoveries and findings, our understanding of the Bible will be very limited.

There is an old Latin saying, "Times change, and we change with them." And this certainly applies to Biblical studies and research. If anyone is unwilling to change, i.e., look at the Gospels and the life of Christ with a different pair of glasses, they will be left in the same spot they have been up until now; they will not advance in a deeper knowledge and understanding of Christianity. Change is not easy, especially as we get older, but refusal to change may lead to devastating affects in our lives depending on circumstances. Refusal to accept change in theology and Biblical studies can leave us spiritually immature and in some cases foolish or naive.

I have no doubt that many Christians will balk at any attempt to change or introduce different concepts about the Bible. I'm sure that you have heard comments like, "That is a sacred book and no one can change it!" I agree, but Biblical research doesn't try to change things as much as it tries to clarify and explain the Bible by digging deeper into its origins and explain what words and expressions meant to the people of those days. Its purpose is to help us understand in a deeper way the true message of Christ today.

None of us is naïve enough to think that times haven't changed. But why do so many think that they can read the Bible just like any other book? We need only look back a few years and see how our lives have changed.

Just a few examples: About a year ago, I met a 26-year old woman who had no idea of what "carbon paper" was. Now that hasn't been gone that long. But suppose she thought that carbon paper was just another kind of wrapping paper and went to the store and bought some carbon paper to wrap a present. Can you imagine what her hands would have looked like after she tried wrapping a gift?

When my daughter was about 10 years of age (some 30 years ago) she couldn't understand that I didn't have television when I was her age.

Back some 65 years ago I remember seeing little round metal ornamental plugs on the walls in some homes. I found out that these plugs covered what used to be gas jets used to light houses before there was electricity.

One of my older brothers told me that when he was younger (back now some 90 years) they did not have a radio and that my Dad had a 'crystal set' to listen to the news.

I bet you can search your memory and find some fantastic inventions that have happened during your life time and now change the way you live. And the speed at which technology is improving, what will life be in just 10 or 20 years from now? Or would you dare to guess farther down the road to 50 years or more?

Well, back to the Bible. When was it written? Some 2,000 years ago? Yes, 2,000 years ago! Do you realize that our country is just a little bit older than 200 years? We need to wait quite a while to add that other "0" and when we do, do you think that any of us (if we were around) would recognize anything around us and how would we understand everything?

Obviously my point is that if things will be so different 1,800 years from now, how different were they back 2,000 years ago? What changes have happened in that span of time that we need to discover in order to understand the meaning of the Bible? It just seems so "common sense" to me!

So if we read the 2,000-year old Bible the same way we read any modern novel or book today, we are bound not to understand it in exactly the same way it was meant when it was written. Just one more example: suppose 200 years from now newspapers don't look like our newspapers today, or that newspapers have disappeared completely, and someone finds a copy of the New York Times newspaper buried in a box. They open the box and read the Times, not knowing that it was a newspaper. How will they understand it?

We can't read the Bible like we read any ordinary book!

So my questions are these; when was printing invented? Who could read and write and when did they learn those abilities? Who taught them? When were eye glasses invented? Who could purchase them? When was electricity invented and who had access to it? How many mistakes in copying did the inscribers make for lack of light and good vision?

Christ died about the year 30 or 33 A.D. The first accounts of His life weren't written until about the year 70. Remember there were no newspapers, or reporters, who started writing down what Jesus did and said. In those days it was the oral transmission of story telling. In fact, various peoples of the earth appointed certain persons in their societies whose main function was to memorize the important events and repeat them when it was necessary. And certainly when Jesus performed a miracle or did or said something that was outstanding or noteworthy, people must have talked among themselves and told and re-told the stories. Do you think each person told the story exactly the same? And don't you think some maybe left out something, added something, or changed something? So by the time His deeds were recorded, there could have been some changes made to the original events that did not drastically change the main story.

And that brings me to another consideration that we have to include. The four Gospels that we know as Matthew, Mark, Luke, and John were not the only Gospels written about Jesus. There are many more – the Gospel of Thomas, Mary, (yes, women had something to say about this Jesus too.), and Judas to mention a few. So what happened to these other writings and why aren't they part of the New Testament?

Try to imagine the early days after Christ disappeared into the Heavens and years after His followers were persecuted. Little by little communities organized themselves and chose leaders and some structure eventually was put into place. Emperors got involved in religion perhaps more for political reasons than for any spiritual advancement. At any rate because of the dispersion of the apostles "to spread the Gospel to all nations", Churches sprung up in the east and the west which were led by different Apostles, who would preach things that they remembered and made decisions, established customs different from one another. We need only to consider the dispute between Peter and Paul about the necessity of the new Christians needing to be circumcised (Galatians 2: 1-21). And finally when the Church began to hold councils to weigh and consider doctrine and organization, they found that they were not all singing out of the same hymnal. There were divisions and differences of opinion and when the Church leaders called for a council between East and West, the West sent more delegates than the East. And, as happens in human affairs, almost all the decisions were those favored by the Western representatives. This is a fact of history and we can not disregard it in trying to reach the full and true meaning of the events that happened over 2,000 years ago. To ignore it is to bury one's head in the sand and say, "No, it never happened. This is God's book and he would not have allowed that to happen." But we have history to prove it did.

The four Gospels that we know today as the New Testament were chosen to be the authentic books of the Bible and the other "gospels" were consider to be "apocryphal" or of questionable authorship of authenticity. (Protestants consider 14 Biblical books included in the Vulgate as "uncanonical" because they are not part of the Hebrew Scriptures. Eleven of these are accepted in the Roman Catholic canon.)

I realize this is an extended introduction, but I feel I would have to address these issues sooner or later. Also, I think these comments will help you better understand from where I am coming.

Part Three

The Bible

Questions

&

Responses

QUESTION #1

The issues of sin and forgiveness are found throughout the Bible, and are frequent themes that are woven into most Christian denominations. Sin is easy to understand since, with the exception of Jesus, it is common to all men. The liturgy of the Lutheran Church includes a prayer during which we quietly confess our sins to God, we repent, and ask for His forgiveness. Speaking for God, the administering pastor acknowledges the forgiveness of our sins. In addition, prior to communion we confess our sins and ask Christ for forgiveness. With faith that Christ took our sins upon Himself, we believe that they are forgiven. On the other hand, some Christians see a more qualified forgiveness, one that acknowledges that God forgives those who truly repent, but that consequences for sins remain. What does the Bible say about the issue?

RESPONSE #1

I have heard ministers who can give a real "fire-hell-and brimstone" sermon on sin, and really scare the listener and make one fearful of dying and eventually facing our Maker. One can not but notice that the Old Testament paints a more severe and stricter God than does the New Testament. My personal view on this is that the Old Testament did not have anyone who could show or demonstrate God's mercy, patience and love as Christ does in the New Testament. The writers of the Old Testament lived under a much more severe and rigid moral code and their writings reflect the same. They were products of their culture and society. Christ came to show us a new way to the Father with the emphasis on compassion, forgiveness and love. And that is a major factor why the establishment couldn't swallow His message of love and forgiveness. He was very, very different from the rest of them.

As evil as sin is, and as hateful and disgusting as it is in the sight of God, the Almighty can clearly distinguish between sin and sinner and while He hates the sin, He does not hate the sinner. I know that is hard to understand because we don't make that distinction so easily in our own personal lives with those who harm us. Most of us probably see the offense and the offender as one and the same. But we can not posit that of God since He is infinite and divine and we are so finite and human. Our God is the most loving, most understanding, most compassionate, and most forgiving Being in all of creation. This does not eradicate the notion of punishment for sin, but it certainly does not overly stress the rigors that some preachers harp upon like doomsday prophets.

I think Christ Himself was aware of this when He said in Matthew 5:17, "Do not think that I have come to abolish the law and the prophets, I have come, not to abolish them, but to fulfill them."

Despite the heavier, somber tone on sin in the Old Testament, we find such passages as Micah 7:18-19. "Who is a God like You, who pardons sin and forgives the transgression of the remnant of His inheritance? You do not stay angry forever but delight to show mercy. You will again have compassion on us; You will tread our sins underfoot and hurl all our iniquities into the depths of the sea." That sounds a bit more like Christ!

Tell me, if our God is not the most compassionate of all beings, how could Christ have come up with a more perfect picture of forgiveness than Matthew 18:21-35?

"Then Peter came to Jesus and asked, 'Lord, how many times shall I forgive my brother when He sins against me? Seven times?' Jesus answered, 'I tell you, not seven times, but seventy-seven times. That is why the kingdom of heaven is like a king who wanted to settle accounts with his servants. As he began the settlement, a man who

owed him a huge amount was brought to him. Since he was not able to pay, the master ordered that he and his wife and his children and all that he had be sold to repay the debt. The servant fell on his knees before him. 'Be patient with me,' he begged, 'and I will pay back everything.' The servant's master took pity on him, canceled the debt and let him go. But when that servant went out, he found one of his fellow servants who owed him a hundred denarii. He grabbed him and began to choke him. 'Pay back what you owe me' he demanded. His fellow servant fell to his knees and begged him, 'Be patient with me, and I will pay you back.' But he refused. Instead, he went off and had the man thrown into prison until he could pay the debt. When the other servants saw what had happened, they were greatly distressed and went and told their master everything that had happened. Then the master called the servant in. 'You wicked servant,' he said, 'I canceled all that debt of yours because you begged me to. Shouldn't you have had mercy on your fellow servant just as I had on you?' In anger his master turned him over to the jailers to be tortured, until he should pay back all he owed. This is how My heavenly Father will treat each of you unless you forgive your brother from your heart."

Christ speaks so much about forgiveness and mercy that it is difficult for me to think that He will treat us otherwise.

How could Jesus who asked for forgiveness for His executioners, be anything than an all-loving, compassionate and merciful judge? "Father, forgive them, for they do not know what they are doing" (Luke 23:34).

QUESTION #2

In several places in the Old Testament, starting with the book of Numbers 14:18 there is similar wording that describes the Lord as being slow to anger, and abounding in steadfast love. What is the explanation for the use of very similar wording by a number of different authors of the books of the Bible? Did they copy each other? Was it a common expression in pre-New Testament days? Did the various writers come up with the same (or very similar) words independently?

RESPONSE #2

Though I do not know the correct explanation for the similarity, it would not at all be surprising to learn that the writers copied each other, or used expressions that were somewhat similar and popular. I'm not saying this was plagiarism, but no doubt they did not have the rules we have today regarding quotations.

QUESTION #3

God was, is, and will forever be the same God. But, there seems to be a difference in the portrayal of God between the Old and New Testaments, with the former showing a more demanding and firm God, as opposed to a more forgiving and loving God in the New Testament. Is there a conflict?

RESPONSE #3

In addition to the following, please refer to my response for Question 1 in this Part.

I don't think there is a conflict so much as there is a different sense of describing God in a more forgiving way. We need only look at Martin Luther King, Mohandas Gandhi, Rosa Parks, Nelson Mandela, and others who have "turned the other cheek" and fought for their causes in a non-violent way. Those ways of responding to civil authorities and making a public statement were unheard of prior to those pioneers. Certainly Christ's style of "turning the other cheek" must have really shocked the old establishment of "an eye for an eye". And just think what it did for pulling out your mule from a ditch on the Sabbath!

Of all the stories in the entire Bible, the one that shows me the greatest differences in portraying God between the Old and New Testament is the story of the Gileadite chieftain, Jephthah. He was the harlot son born to Gilead and some years later the elders chose Jephthah to lead them in battle against their enemy, the Ammonites. Before engaging in battle, however, "Jephthah made a vow to the Lord. 'If you deliver the Ammonites into my power,' he said, 'whoever comes out of the doors of my house to meet me when I return in triumph from the Ammonites shall belong to the Lord. I shall offer him up as a holocaust." (Judges 11: 30, 31) (A rather strange way to honor the Lord, I would think.) At any rate, Jephthah wins an astounding victory conquering twenty cities in all. And when he returns to his home "it was his daughter who came forth, playing the tambourines and dancing. She was an only child. When he saw her, he rent his garments and said, 'Alas, daughter, you have struck me down and brought calamity upon me. For I have made a vow to the Lord and I cannot retract.' Her father "...did to her as he had vowed" (Judges 11:39).

To me this portrays a very cold, insensitive, stark sense of justice totally devoid of any mercy, understanding, or compassion. It totally ignores the value of life – innocent life at that – because of a promise or vow made most probably with great emotions (only the heart without the head) and fervor for doing battle to the hated enemy. There is no after thought that, "Hey, maybe God doesn't expect me to carry out this foolish idea after all. I'll go and kill a goat or calf or something else because I never really had in mind to kill a person, much less my own daughter. Certainly God doesn't expect me to kill my own daughter!"

I guess this hits home particularly deep for me because as a professed religious person I made a vow of chastity for life and as a priest took an oath of celibacy. Yet, circumstances changed during my life that led me to seek and obtain dispensations from both the vow and oath through official Church authorities. And there are thousands of others like me who have done the same. Is God angry with us? I prayed and sought counsel before making my decisions which I do not regret nor fear punishment from God for doing so.

QUESTON #4

In the Apostle's Creed there are two issues that I've pondered. First, "---the resurrection of the body" (I would think that it's the soul that leaves the body). The body changes over time, so which body would go to heaven? Second, "---he descended into hell---". I would think that God would have immediately embraced Christ. What am I failing to understand?

RESPONSE #4

The soul indeed leaves the body and death results. Catholic teaching always referred to the "glorified" body as the resurrected body. That would mean that no matter in what condition the person was when He died, our resurrected body would be a complete healthy body. Since this has not happened to anyone yet, as far as I know, we can only conjecture as to what happens.

"He descended into hell" in Catholic theology means that after Christ's death on the cross, He visited the souls of the just who were awaiting His redeeming death. Since He had not gained heaven for

them before His death they could not enter heaven until He had accomplished His sacrifice on the cross. I do not know how other faiths understand this phrase.

QUESTION #5

Being gripped with fear, it seems that the apostles deserted Christ at His crucifixion. Did they eventually accomplish His will? If yes in what way was it done?

RESPONSE #5

I think we would have to answer with a definite "yes" that they did eventually accomplish His will since, according to tradition, all of them but John died a martyrs' death. It would seem that Christ's own words, "There is no greater love than this: to lay down one's life for one's friend" (John 15:13) should be taken as His personal approval of the apostles having accomplished His will.

QUESTION #6

Since the Bible was written at a time and in a culture that is now viewed by some as being out of date, does it still have the same relevance to the twenty-first century world?

RESPONSE #6

As I mentioned in my introductory remarks, we can't read the Bible as any ordinary book. It is not a history book, it is not a science book, it is not a novel, and it is not fiction. It is a sacred and holy document filled with many stories, allegories, accounts of the times in which it was written in order to teach people every where how to live one's life for peace and harmony in this world and for everlasting life with our Creator in the next world. Is it out of date? Some of the stories and examples are and that is why we need biblical research that we spoke about earlier to understand what is the message for us today. Parts of the Bible, mainly from the Old Testament, are out of date because the references describe human wars and political events that have passed and have no relevancy to today except the lessons that may be learned from some of these events.

QUESTION #7

Did all commandments from God stop after the writing of the Bible?

RESPONSE #7

That depends what you mean by "commandments"? Did God give us more commandments like the "Ten Commandments"? No. Are there other written exhortations, counsels, advice, instructions, suggestions that we should heed for our own spiritual good? Yes, and then there are the individual promptings of the spirit within our souls that only each one of us can hear and answer. "The wind blows where it will. You hear the sound it makes but you do not know where it comes from, or where it goes. So it is with everyone begotten of the Spirit." (John 3:8)

QUESTION #8

On occasion, I find myself trying to reconcile the commandment from Christ, "Do not judge, or you too will be judged", with the everyday need to make judgments. We are constantly faced with the choice of good or bad, right or wrong, yes or no issues relating to other people. If we did not make decisions we might well be encouraging evil or issues in conflict with Christian beliefs. How do we reconcile this potential conflict?

RESPONSE #8

I don't think that the command not to judge another applies to all our judgments about others. We judge all day long. "He is talking." "She is smiling." "The sky is blue." You may say that these are statements, and they are. But in philosophy they are known as judgments. Each time we posit (put forward as a fact) one thing of another that is a judgment. So those are judgments, but they are not moral judgments. Now if you see me some night in a very dim, romantic restaurant with a woman whom you definitely know is not my wife, you can still make a judgment (in fact, you have to unless you want to deny your vision) that you saw me in a restaurant with a woman who was not my wife. That too is a judgment, but if you infer something more than that from seeing me with her, then we are talking about moral judgment. The woman could be my sister, niece, or anyone except what may pop up in most people's mind. And then we could be talking about gossip, slander, and calumny and why are they so evil.

And you are correct, we need to make judgments everyday, not only because we are constantly faced with choices of good or bad, etc. Not making decisions could encourage evil. Take a court judge. He is making judgments all the time. That is his duty. Not to make judgments when they should, judges would be derelict in their duties. This same principle can be applied to parents, teachers, and other leaders in our society who have an obligation to nurture, instruct, counsel, etc. others. For these folks not to judge at times could very well mean sinning by omission.

So the command not to judge should not to be taken in an absolute sense like "never, never judge!". This is a good example why it is important to understand the Bible and not just read the words and take them on their face value.

QUESTION #9

Even though I spent most of my career associated with the military, I've often wondered about the role of Christianity in time of war. Some say that religion is one of the main causes of war. But, looking back on the history of the United States, our wars were often fought with Christians on both sides. In the Civil War we even saw a leading Confederate general, Leonidas Polk, who had been the Episcopal bishop in the South prior to the war. In both WWI and WWII we fought Germany which had deep Christian roots. How do we reconcile our obedience to God and at the same time engage in killing of other Christians?

RESPONSE #9

There is no doubt that our civil authorities have their command to rule and govern society through the power that God places in the rightful power of the individual states and countries. These entities must answer to God for the way they rule and for their treatment of the citizens. I think we reconcile our obedience to God by our respect and faithful adherence to those just laws and practices of our legitimately elected leaders. That is why the role of politics should be treated so much more seriously than it is today. Politics and governing should not be seen as an area excluded from our moral responsibilities. If we treat politics like we treat rooting for our favorite football team, we are not being fully responsible as Christians.

How do we reconcile killing anyone whether Christian or not? Your question brings us back to the question of a "just war". When is it just and who makes that decision?

When Christ was asked if it is lawful to pay taxes, he responded, "...give to Caesar what is Caesar's, but give to God what is God's (Matthew 22; 21). This same text is often cited for other obligations to the state. It doesn't mean that the state is higher than the spiritual world; in fact, the spiritual demands supersede earthly demands, but do not abolish them. So if we are to be both loyal citizens and good Christians, we have an obligation to support and sustain the common good determined by those whom we have legitimately elected to governor us. The issues over which wars are fought may, and often do, have spiritual overtones, but the decisions to go to war are not religious ones today. There is nothing in Christianity that says that all Christians must subscribe to the same economic policies. Far from it; look at our own country, we have Christians on both sides (and in the middle) of every single political issue regardless if the issue be remotely or closely aligned with religious overtones.

The command not to kill is one of the most serious commands that God has given. God is the author and giver of life and decides when life ends for any one of us. However, it is theologically understood that for the common good of society the state legitimately shares in the responsibilities of administering justice among its citizens. This includes not only the right to make laws, but also includes the state's obligation to protect and defend its people. The principles of self-defense and just wars must be seriously weighed by everyone concerned when laws are made and enacted that concern society.

QUESTION #10

The essence of Christianity would seem to be deeply, if not mostly, tied to the resurrection. Given its extraordinarily strong position in our faith, what are the events that led the Apostles and others to not only accept the miracle, but to go forward and commit their lives to Christ as a result of their witnessing the resurrection?

RESPONSE #10

Some of the events that led the Apostles and others to accept the miracle of the resurrection can be found in the Gospels themselves, such as the women at the tomb in Mark 16, and Jesus' appearance to the Apostles after the resurrection in Luke 24 as well as in John 21. We can also find post-resurrection accounts in the Acts of the Apostles and in some of the epistles of Paul, Peter, James, John, Jude, and the Book of Revelation. And no doubt there were other incidents that have not been recorded. I have no proof for my belief, just my own personal thought.

While at the time of Christ's crucifixion the apostles were full of fear and too afraid to appear in public because they were known as His followers; after the resurrection everything changed for them. They not only bravely recruited and filled Judas' position (Acts 1:21), they began to preach boldly after the descent of the Holy Spirit (Acts 2) in the streets and synagogues and ignored the prohibitions not to preach in Jesus' name or about Him. In the entire Acts of the Apostle, Luke supplements his Gospel with a second volume describing the origin and spread of the Christian communities in New Testament times. This account provides a broad survey of the church's development from the resurrection of Jesus to Paul's first Roman imprisonment.

The importance of the Resurrection for Christians can be summed up in Paul's own words, "And if Christ has not been raised, our preaching is void of content and your faith is empty too. (1Corinthians 15:14)" and "if Christ was not raised, your faith is worthless...and those who have fallen asleep in Christ are the deadest of the dead. If our hopes in Christ are limited to this life only; we are the most pitiable of men (and women)" (1 Corinthians 15:17-19).

QUESTION #11

What is known about Christ's life during the period from His birth until His ministry?

RESPONSE #11

Not much except what we read in the four Gospels. As I mentioned above, the other "gospels" also offer some insights about Jesus. Reading books by reputable Scripture scholars can shed some light about the times in which Christ lived and give us a better understanding of what His life was like. Such reading can be interesting by helping us to understand the times of Christ in a more realistic and less romanticized way.

QUESTION #12

The Bible speaks about eternity. Since we're programmed to think in terms of time, distance, and space, eternity is a hard concept to grasp. Is there an explanation that would help us to understand something that has no limits?

RESPONSE #12

There are probably hundreds of explanations to help us understand eternity. One early one I remember goes like this: Imagine an iron ball the size of the earth and once every hundred years a bird flies around the ball and with its feathers knocks off a speck of the iron dust. When the ball of iron is finally gone, eternity hasn't even begun. And I'm sure you can match that one.

In his second letter St Peter (3:8) says, "In the Lord's eyes, one day is as a thousand years and a thousand years are as a day." It should be noted here that St. Peter isn't saying that with God one day is (or equals) a thousand years and a thousand years is (or equals) a day. He is saying it is "as" or "like" a thousand years. He used a figure of speech, a simile, to compare a day to a thousand years. Perhaps it's comparable to when we are 12 years of age, we think people 50 and 60 are old. And when we get to 50 or 60 we say, "Where did the years go?"

QUESTION #13

In Genesis 1:26 it is stated, "Then God said, "Let us make man in our image---". Why is there a plural reference with the use of "us" and our?

RESPONSE #13

There are no simple, quick answers to this question. You can find treatises on Hebrew grammar and all kinds of interpretations as to whether this refers to the Trinity or was this a result of grammatical errors, etc., etc. Some say that since God's creation of man was his greatest act of creation, He took all the best of what He had already created, added to it and made man. So, God was really speaking to all the animals and everything else that He had created and that is why the plural is used. You will find other explanations, but none of them support the idea that there is more than one God.

Another consideration which I did not touch upon in my preamble is that there was no one single author of the Bible. Remember, there was an oral tradition first and then people began to write it down and others copied it and, no doubt changes were made with no maliciousness on anyone's part, just human error.

It is interesting that after "Let us make man in our image, after our likeness…"in (Genesis 1: 26) we find in the very next verse, (27), "God created man in His image; in the divine image He created him; …" There is no plural. It appears that verse 27 is probably older than verse 26 according to scholars.

We need only read other parts of the Bible and nowhere else is there any hint that God is not one. Deuteronomy 6: 4 says, "The Lord our God is ONE."

QUESTION #14

In Philippians 3:8, Paul makes reference to everything else being a loss when compared to the greatness of knowing Christ. How would you define "knowing Christ"?

RESPONSE # 14

I'm sure you've heard the phrase at Christmas time, "Jesus is the reason for the season." I think it would be good to post a sign like "Jesus is the reason." on our desks, on our mirrors, in our cars, and other prominent places all year round where it would serve as a constant reminder of what it is all about.

I think I know Christ the person, first, from the New Testament, then I know Him best in trying to see Him in myself as I interact with others, and also in others with whom I come in contact as I go through life. Some of those encounters last a long time and many come and go as I live out my daily life. In my daily life I try to imitate the sentiments of Paul "...and the life I live now is not my own; Christ is living in me. I still live my human life, but it is a life of faith in the Son of God, who loved me and gave Himself for me" (Galatians 2:20). I say that I try, some times it is only a feeble try, but I have trust in the goodness of God to know that I am trying. That is all he asks – that we try.

QUESTION #15

In 1 John 2:15 it's stated that "Love not the world, neither the things that are in the world. If any man loves the world, the love of the Father is not in him." But, if God created the world and man to live in it, is it not appropriate to love God's creation?

RESPONSE #15

Yes, indeed we are supposed to love God's creation...all of it, because as Genesis tells us that after God created "God saw how good it was" (Genesis 1:10). But the "world" that Christ is referring to in John 2:15 is not the physical earth, but the evils in the world – the injustices, hatred, stealing, criticism, arrogance, deception, lies, murders, prejudice, and every other kind of sin. That is the world – the evil empire of the devil who doesn't tire of trying to snatch us in his grasp. That is why we read, "Stay sober and alert. Your opponent the devil is prowling like a roaring lion looking for someone to devour" (1Peter 5:8). And "For these I pray – not for the world...I am in the world no more, but these are in the world as I come to You...

(John 17:9). Again, "I gave them Your word and the world has hated them for it; they do not belong to the world any more than I belong to the world. I do not ask You to take them out of the world, but to guard them from the evil one (John 17:14). And again, "They are not of the world any more than I belong to the world" (John 17:14-16).

"Do not conform yourselves to this world, but be transformed by the renewal of your minds, so that you may judge what is God's will, what is good, pleasing and perfect" (Romans 12:2). Be in the world, but not of the world! "If you belonged to the world, it would love you as it own; the reason it hates you is that you do not belong to the world. But I chose you out of the world" (John 15:18-19).

The dictionary defines "worldly" as "of, pertaining to, or devoted to the temporal world; not spiritual or religious; secular." Another meaning is "sophisticated or cosmopolitan; worldly-wise". The use of the word "worldly" was common parlance among religious orders of men and women. When I was in the seminary, especially the novitiate (a year of intense spiritual formation before taking temporary vows) the "Novice Master," as he was called, drilled us on not being "worldly". This meant that we were not to be preoccupied with material things; not seeking the nicest things in life, like clothing and food, or the most comfortable surroundings. We were to always be neat and clean in our appearance and clothing and maintain our rooms in good order. Our rule book reminded us that "cleanliness was next to godliness". Flashy clothing was very unbecoming as was loud and boisterous music or behavior. We were to avoid having any very special interests in movies, secular magazines, television and other "worldly" distractions. We were to concentrate on our spiritual lives and avoid those things that would distract us, or to learn how to use them in moderation. Of course, seminary life was like living in a bubble of protection from "the outside world". But it was an intense training whose purpose was to help us establish habits that would serve us well in the real world of the ministry where we continued to develop a taste for things spiritual and little by little not let the influence of the "world" infiltrate our thinking so that we could develop and deepen our own spiritual lives by concentrating more easily on the things of God. Keeping in tune with the "world" was seen as an obstacle to developing a deep sensitivity to ones spiritual life.

QUESTION #16

I recall that Jesus helped us to understand His message with His answer to the question as to whether there is one thing more important than the rest. In response He stated that we should love God above all else and our neighbor as ourselves. With that simplicity, I wonder if there aren't too many other distractions that complicate our understanding. Should there be more emphasis placed on that message?

RESPONSE #16

Yes, there are plenty of other distractions that complicate our understanding of what is THE most important thing in life. We already discussed Christ's response about love of God and neighbor being the most important issue of His message. We heard Him tell the young man, "If you seek perfection, go, sell your possessions, and give to the poor. You will then have treasure in heaven. Afterward, come back and follow Me"(Matthew 19: 21). And, "Wherever your treasure lies, there your heart will be" (Luke 12:34).

Yes, if we are serious about being a true follower of Christ, then we need to take an inventory of where we stand from time to time regarding how we are practicing His message. We need to concentrate on the essentials – love of God and neighbor. Some people make a spiritual retreat once a year for this purpose. I think an excellent place to focus our attention is found in Matthew 25, 35 – 45, (sometimes entitled 'the last judgment') only because I think it spells out for Christians in great detail what Christ means by loving our neighbor. "I was hungry ...thirsty...a stranger...naked...ill...in prison...and you helped Me..." We refer to these as the corporal works of mercy, but they are the acts on which our eternal salvation rests. How well or poorly we responded to these needs of our neighbor during our life time will determine our fate. God has given us the blueprint for our salvation. It is not too complicated or difficult. We just have to be willing to accept it.

But I suggest that we update Christ's list, and make it as meaningful as we can in the 21st century. Will His words sound something like "I was poor; illegal; uneducated; homeless; unemployed; gay; bullied; abused; etc, etc...and you ministered to Me?" Could the list even include how we treat those who belong to different religious faiths, or even different political parties, or family members who we find annoying for whatever reason? You can become creative and come up with your own list, I'm sure.

*One interesting note about these corporal works of mercy is that Christ doesn't say anything about **why** the person is in prison, or **why** they are hungry, naked, or ill, etc. He simply points out that the person is in need of assistance. Being a genuine Christian requires us to go beyond just keeping the Ten Commandments. It even means more than just doing what is deemed by society as legally and morally correct. We can't live the life of Christ by being legalists or moralist just trying to avoid sin. We have to go far beyond that and walk the extra mile by sharing our coat with those out in the cold, defending those abused by others, inconveniencing ourselves to assist those less fortunate than ourselves, etc., etc. Imitate the Good Samaritan (Luke 10:25-37); he went beyond the law and showed compassion. Remember, every time we neglect or refuse* *to carry out these corporal works of mercy, we have denied doing it to Christ.*

Should there be more emphasis placed on that message, you asked. Could you imagine the kind of world, or country, we would be living in if this message of Christ was our guide?

QUESTION #17

When Christ came on earth there were people throughout the world, but there was no communication through the Bible, or even awareness in the areas outside easy reach by crude sailing ships or walking. From the seed planted by Christ through the Apostles His word eventually permeated most of the world over the next 2000 years. But, even today there are people who have never been exposed to God through Christ. How are these souls viewed by God?

RESPONSE #17

I may have touched upon this in one of earlier responses.

No one knows how these souls are viewed by God, but the common belief in Catholic theology is that these souls are left to the mercy of God. That may sound like a cop-out, but to say that they are saved the same way as those who know Christ would encourage others not to worry about trying to follow Christ. And to say they are damned would be pretty judgmental of God not being merciful since these souls never knew Christ. We are mere mortal people and we do not fully know the mind of God, especially what plans he has for these souls.

QUESTION #18

Few, if any, passages in the Bible are as well known as John 3:16. The example of God's love for us that it represents is hard for humans to comprehend. It's the ultimate of an outstretched hand from God that we should all eagerly embrace and give thanks. What should we consider, and how should we respond to this ultimate act of love?

RESPONSE #18

Yes, "John 3:16" is a very famous passage, one you even see held up among the crowds in ball parks.

I feel like I got a little "preachy" in my response to your Question 15 above and may have thought I was up in a pulpit of past years! So, I'm a little hesitant to beat the same drum over and over again even though I believe that the central doctrine of Christianity can not be over-emphasized.

If you want to read a love story, read John 14 through 17. There Jesus speaks His last discourse with His disciples before His death. I call your attention in particular to Chapter 15, verses 12 to17 – "This is My commandment: love one another as I have loved you. There is no greater love than this; to lay down one's life for one's friends. You are My friends if you do what I command you...The command I give you is this, that you love one another."

They often refer to the youngest apostle, John, as the apostle whom Christ loved more than the others. I don't know if that is true, but none of them spoke as elegantly as John about love. For example, "If anyone says, 'My love is fixed on God,' yet hates his brother (or sister), he is a liar. One who has no love for the brother (or sister) he has seen cannot love the God he has not seen. The commandment we have from Him is this: whoever loves God must also love his brother (and sister)" (2John:4, 20-21).

No one – NO ONE – could make the message clearer than that! There are NO conditions put on God's love and NO conditions can be put on our love for one another.

QUESTION #19

At the root of Christian/Judaic religion are the Ten Commandments given to Moses by God. It would be hard to argue against the divinely inspired wisdom that has enabled them to remain the cornerstone of our world for thousands of years. But, so many new religious sects have come into being with their own emphasis on what compliance is required that it's hard to know what is critical and directly related to the obedience and glorification of God. How do we determine what was divinely commanded by God?

RESPONSE #19

Our basis for what is required of us as Christians is found in the Bible. For those of other faiths, they must in good conscience follow what they believe is the revealed truth for them. God is not going to judge us Christians based solely on the Old Testament which did not know Christ, or on the Buddhist, Hindu, or Muslim beliefs anymore than He is going to judge them on Christian beliefs. And for those new religious sects that have come into being with their own emphasis on what compliance is required, they will have to answer to God for their beliefs. I don't usually listen to these preachers, but every now and then I will catch bits and pieces of their preaching. Some are very good motivational speakers, have large followings and can give some good insights into living a better life, even a better spiritual life. They try to keep everything positive and it almost sounds like a positive mental attitude training session which isn't bad, but rather devoid of religion. You have probably noticed that many of these programs purposely lack any sign or symbol of anything religious in any way. But what I notice missing is any reference to sin and the obligation to follow God's will which means that we need to concentrate on Jesus' message. You may feel good after listening to the program, but does it teach you how to love God and your neighbor?

QUESTION #20

The existence (or non-existence) of hell is a controversial issues among many Christians. At the core of the controversy is the conflict between God and the devil. If God is omnipotent, almighty, loving and creator of all that is seen and unseen, one might justifiably think that everything else is subordinate to his wishes.

We have all witnessed people who by our worldly definition and common sense are evil and unfit to live in a civilized society. Some may be mentally ill, others may have made the worst possible decisions due to a lack of training, education or nurturing. But, surely there are some who we might say (for lack of a more detailed explanation) are just bad, rotten and ruthless. and without any apparent value. Society, in its less than perfect worldly manner, attempts to deal with these people through our judicial system. Within the context of this issue is the obvious recognition of free will and consequence for personal actions. But, there isn't always an even playing field for the exercise of free will. Would our heavenly Father condemn one of his children to an eternal hell? What is hell, and who will likely be its inhabitants?

RESPONSE #20

You ask some difficult questions!

I don't think that our Heavenly Father condemns anyone to eternal hell. The individual person decides that for himself. Just think of a human judge passing sentence. I'm not saying that the human judge will not make a mistake. Of course, that can happen from time to time, and has. And there have been some pretty unfair and unjust sentences passed out by human judges in our history. But would a human judge condemn a person to death or life in prison, say for stealing a car, or domestic violence? Probably not!

God is not going to condemn anyone to hell unless (1) the sin is a serious violation of His law; (2) the sinner has full knowledge of the seriousness of the sin; (3) the sinner gives full consent to violating the law, and (4) remains unrepentant for committing the offense.

What is hell? We don't know. There are those who believe that we make our own hell right here on earth!

There are several passages in the New Testament which speak of "weeping and gnashing of teeth." "And I say unto you, that many shall come from the east and west, and shall sit down with Abraham, and Isaac, and Jacob, in the kingdom of heaven. But the children of the kingdom shall be cast out into outer darkness: there shall be weeping and gnashing of teeth "(Matthew 8: 11-12). Other citations are Matthew 13: 41-42; 13: 49-50; 22:12-13: Luke 13: 27-28 and other places.

Who will likely be its inhabitants? I am not sure, I think it will most probably include those who failed to carry out the will of God; those who heard the message of the importance of love of God and love of neighbor, but didn't pay any attention to it.

If I may once again return to the last judgment and the corporal works of mercy that we spoke about in Question 15, we find Christ talking about the second group of people (the goats) in Matthew 25: 41-46 who did not attend to the needs of others and says that when the Son of Man comes in His glory, "...He will say to those on His left: 'Out of my sight, you condemned, into that everlasting fire prepared for the devil and his angels! I was hungry and you gave Me no food, I was thirsty and you gave Me no drink. I was away from home and you gave Me no welcome, naked and you gave Me no clothing, I was ill and in prison and you did not come to comfort Me." Then they in turn will ask: 'Lord, when did we see You hungry or thirsty or away from home or naked or ill or in prison and not attend You in Your needs?' He will answer them: 'I assure you, as often as you neglected to do it to one of these least ones, you neglected to do it to Me. These will go off to eternal punishment and the just to eternal life."

QUESTION #21

As I read Luke 16 about the dishonest steward who wasted his master's goods, and then went about to protect his future in a less than ethical manner, I found it hard to grasp the intended lesson. By commending the steward it would seem that it encouraged bad behavior. What should I have learned from that story, and how does it apply to the current world?

RESPONSE #21

No, I don't think this parable is so much about encouraging bad behavior, as it is to show how shrewd people are about worldly affairs. Christ says the steward was dishonest and even speaks of his act as "wickedness". But Christ points out that he was "shrewd". The implication being that if we can be that shrewd about material possessions, how much more prudent and solicitous should we be in pursuing spiritual riches. Jesus doesn't applaud dishonesty, but shows to what lengths wicked people will go in seeking material riches.

Christ also points out that if we can be trusted in small matters, we will be trusted with larger matters, and if we are dishonest with small things, we will be dishonest with greater things. The implication is, how do we handle all that has been given to us – large or small – our talents, gifts, responsibilities at work and at home as spouses, parents, children, neighbors, citizens, etc.

QUESTION #22

I can remember being an eleven-year old Boy Scout and learning the Scout Oath which includes the words---cheerful, thrifty, **brave**--- . Brave was defined as standing up for righteousness even when it's unpopular and not in conformance with the view of the majority. While not easy to do, it would appear to be in compliance with the teaching of the Lord. Are there examples in the scripture that talk to this issue?

RESPONSE #22

I know the word "righteousness" is used frequently, especially among Protestant denominations, and the dictionary defines "righteous" as "meeting the standard of what is right" and only notes that "righteousness" is a noun. "Righteousness" for Catholics means "justice". I have read some articles by Protestant writers who seem to defend the word "righteousness" as meaning something more than "justice". I fail to see the difference. But I think I can still answer your question even with this difference in the exact meaning.

I can relate to "brave" being defined as "standing up for what is just even when it's unpopular..." And, of course, that is never easy to do especially when doing so may make you unpopular or stick out in the crowd, or have more serious consequences.

We have been speaking of what it means to be a Christian today. So look at how many times we have seen on the news how some poor, helpless person, was attacked by someone while others just stood around and watched, or walked away without even calling for help.

I think when Christ defended the woman caught in adultery (John 8:1-11) He demonstrated what it meant to be just and forgiving. He came to her defense and did not allow them to kill her by stoning her. Don't you think there were some in the crowd who criticized Him for that? Did He care? I think that we can say that in many of the miracles recorded in the Gospels, Christ was moved not only by compassion, but by a sense of justice to establish the status quo for those afflicted. I think you will see that in the story of the paralytic, (John 5); the man born blind, (John 9); the man with the withered hand, (Matthew 12: 9-13); or any of His other miracles.

QUESTION #23

As indicated in a previous question, when compared with the New Testament, the Old Testament appears to be harsher in its tone. As examples, in Exodus 32:25-30 Moses brings about the killing of 3000 people in the name of the Lord. Then, Joshua follows in the footsteps of Moses with further acts of extreme violence when he aggressively slaughters the occupants of lands that it says were promised to the Israelites. To what can we attribute the wrath of God that would bring about such massive killing of all occupants, including the women and children?

RESPONSE #23

I don't know if we can rightly attribute the wrath of God for such deeds in the Old Testament even though it is portrayed as such. I hope I do not repeat myself too much from what I have previously said on this subject.

But we have to remember that the writers of the Bible were human beings – whoever they were – they were not supernatural spirits devoid of bodies and all those lesser instincts that go with humanity. We should remember that folks back in the olden times could sometimes act in ways that seem rather short of savagery to us. We do not even have to go back to Biblical times to find a display of some horrendous inhuman acts. Look at some of the stories of the Middle Ages - burnings at the stake, beheadings, the Crusades, and other terrible wars, and the like...all this supposedly done in the name of God? I don't think so! And then let's fast forward to more modern times and still today in the Middle East we see some terribly inhuman forms of torture and punishment against prisoners of war and some non-prisoners, even beheadings today.

My point is that those writers of the Old Testament could easily imagine that if their kings and society condoned such terrible acts, God, the almighty king, could do no less.

I bother very little as to why God was so terribly described in the Old Testament, because I firmly believe that the loving, compassionate, just, and forgiving Father/Mother that Jesus Christ has revealed to us will be my counselor, defender and judge without any of those horrible attributes shown in the Old Testament..

QUESTION #24

When looking at Christianity, can it be said that the effect of Christ on the world was greater after the resurrection, or was it His message and teaching while on earth. Or, should we not try to separate them?

RESPONSE #24

I have no idea how one could measure the two. But it would seem to me that the effect of Christ on the world was greater after the resurrection since a longer period of time has past since the resurrection and more people have heard His message. We need to consider how communications have changed since Christ's time alone. I don't see what is to be gained by trying to separate them, but it is an interesting question.

QUESTON #25

Most people fear death, probably because of the unknown. But, to some extent, it's also likely to be due to a lack of faith. What can we do as Christians to ease that fear?

RESPONSE #25

I have a dear friend in Scotland who says she believes her dying day will be the most beautiful day of her life.

Just recently a religious brother whom I knew for over 60 years passed away. On his dying bed he turned to a friend with a smile and said, "I didn't think that leaving would be so beautiful."

These are people of faith who have lived their lives as Christ wanted. I believe their words and feelings will be the same for all who do likewise.

Fear of the unknown can cause anxiety and I don't think that some fear of dying is unchristian; it's just normal and natural. But we should have a firm trust in the Lord that – if we have lived our lives as He has directed us to the best of our abilities – we have nothing to fear. Once again we turn to Matthew (25:34) and find Christ speaking of the last judgment, "Come. You have my Father's blessing. Inherit the kingdom prepared for you from the creation of the world." In John (14:1-3) "Do not let your hearts be troubled. Have faith in God and faith in Me. In my Father's house there are many dwelling places; otherwise, how could I have told you that I was going to prepare a place for you? I am indeed going to prepare a place for you and then I shall come back to take you with Me, that where I am you also may be. You know the way that leads where I go."

And every Christian knows the story of the raising of Lazarus (John 11:1-43). Christ tells Martha and Mary, "I am the resurrection and the life: whoever believes in Me, though he should die, will come to life; and whoever is alive and believes in Me will never die" (John 11:25-26).

There are so many beautiful references to death and the afterlife in Scripture that it is hard to pick the most meaningful. I'll list a few here. "Eye has not seen, ear has not heard, nor has it so much as dawned on man what God has prepared for those who love Him" (1 Corinthians 2:9).

"The souls of the just are in the hands of God, and no torment shall touch them They seemed in the view of the foolish to be dead; and their passing away was thought an affliction and their going forth from us utter destruction. But they are at peace"(Wisdom 3:1-3).

"If we have died with Christ, we believe we shall also live with Him. We know that Christ, raised from the dead, dies no more; death no longer has power over Him" (Romans 6:8-9).

"What will separate us from the love of Christ? Will anguish or distress or persecution or famine or nakedness or peril or the sword? No, in all things we conquer overwhelmingly through God who loved us. For I am convinced that neither death, nor life, nor angels, nor principalities, nor the present things, nor future things will be able to separate us from the love of God in Christ Jesus" (Romans 8:31-37).

And one more...

"We know that if our earthly dwelling, a tent, should be destroyed, we have a building from God, a dwelling not made with hands, eternal in heaven. So we are always courageous" (Corinthians 5:6-8).

QUESTION #26

In our current politically correct world, how should we view Paul's statement in 1 Timothy 2:11, which states "Let a woman learn in silence with all submissiveness. I permit no woman to teach or to have authority over men; she is to keep silent. For Adam was formed first, then Eve; and Adam was not deceived, but the woman was deceived and became a transgressor. Yet woman will be saved through bearing children, if she continues in faith and love and holiness, with modesty".

The relationship between men and women in today's western culture, particularly in the United States, is one of sharing, equality, and mutual respect. Spanning the spectrum of society from marriage, professions, the military, business, and even captured in Federal law as related to non-discrimination, woman are neither silent or submissive. Your thoughts?

RESPONSE #26

Earlier, I addressed some of my thoughts about equality for women and that response should be considered here as well.

We have to remember that Paul was a human being, a victim of his environment and his times just as any of us today are of ours. At one time he persecuted Christians and stoned them to death. The Acts of the Apostles clearly identifies Paul (then Saul) involved in some way in the death of the first Christian martyr, Stephen. Describing Stephen's death, the author of Acts says, "The onlookers were shouting aloud, holding their hands over their ears as they did so. Then they rushed at him as one man, dragged him out of the city, and began to stone him. The witnesses meanwhile were piling their cloaks at the feet of a young man named Saul" (Acts7:57-58).

Paul preached other things that we can and should correctly challenge, i.e., slavery..."Slaves, obey your human masters with the reverence, the awe, and the sincerity you owe to Christ..."(Ephesians 6:5). How can we defend that today where we have learned that "all men and woman are created equal"? He also gives women an exhortation in 1 Corinthians 14:33-36 as follows, "...woman should keep silent in such gatherings. They may not speak...as the law states, submissiveness is indicated for them. If they want to learn anything, they should ask their husbands at home..." And in 1 Timothy 2:11 we find, "A woman must learn in silence and be completely submissive. I do not permit a woman to act as teacher."

All I can say is "Poor Paul"! He knew a lot about the spiritual life of Christ, but he was a stranger to the powerful gifts and talents that God has given to women. The world certainly has changed since Paul's time regarding the status of woman – thank God! How enriched we are as people because of the great women the world has known in every walk of life. Just think what our world would be today if we had followed Paul's advice about not allowing a woman to act as a teacher. How many men and women today owe a great part of their education to a woman? And I will not even mention all the different positions that women have filled in our world since Paul's times. We had to wait until President Lincoln to abolish slavery in our country. It is no surprise that we had to wait much longer to grant equality to women. So while we do not condemn Paul for his views on women, we certainly do pardon his ignorance in the name of Christ. I often wonder if Paul ever stopped to think of the role that the Blessed Virgin Mary played in the life of Jesus Christ. Wasn't it sort of pivotal? How did he view her? I could go on, but I better get to your next question.

QUESTION #27

Most Christians believe that the Bible was influenced by the Holy Spirit. But, there doesn't seem to be a common agreement on how that should be viewed. Some would say that every word is literally accurate. Then there are those who believe that while it is divinely inspired it has been altered by time, the human element, the efforts in translation, and the ability of the reader to understand the context within which some statements are made. And, then there are those who attribute a disproportionate emphasis to certain verses or words.

Who actually wrote the Bible (Old and New Testament) and when? How close to the original work is what is we read today in English? How should we view the content of the Bible?

RESPONSE #27

I think I mentioned that you ask some difficult questions, didn't I? Well, to get the full answer to this question, you will need to enroll in a Bible course.

Before I go on to respond to your question, I think my response to your Question # 26 is a perfect example of what you are referring to in this question and my earlier comment why the Bible can not be read like any other book. Paul was no authority on human rights and equality of the sexes, and he didn't receive any special inspiration from God about how to deal with slavery and women and a lot of other subjects. So no one can quote the Bible as an authority for every single thing that is mentioned therein. I think this emphasizes the point which you make in the Preface of this book. People need guidance in interpreting the Bible.

I hope I don't disappoint you by saying that there are many, many human authors of the Bible. There would have to be since the Old and New Testaments cover such an enormous number of years from creation to the Resurrection of Christ.

There is no denying that Moses had a role in the development of the Pentateuch – the first five books of the Bible. He is not conceived of as the author of the books in the modern sense, but he had a uniquely important role as lawgiver. However, there were several (at least four) other historical traditions and sources also involved and each shows its own characteristics, its own theological view point, and creates a rich variety of interpretations. What this means is that "the reader is not held to undeviating literalness in interpreting the words, 'the Lord said to Moses'. One must keep in mind that the Pentateuch is the crystallization of Israel's age-old relationship with God." (The New American Bible: Introduction to the Pentateuch) So now, are you ready to go through each book?

To answer your question properly we would have to go book by book unless you expected me to say that God is the author because He inspired the writers. But then we would have a very long discussion about what "inspiration" means to different Scripture scholars and theologians. Does inspiration mean that God inspire every single word that each author used, or does it mean God inspired the thought and left the writer to use his own words?

Again, I don't let myself get all tied up in questions of this nature because I don't see too much value in it for me where I am at this stage of my life. I believe in the Bible as the Word of the Lord and from it I learn how I have to live my life, treat others, and trust in God.

I hope you don't consider that a flippant answer or unprofessional, but life looks different to me now than it did 45 years ago. You know, Ernie, even as a priest, I never tried to convert anyone to Catholicism. I hope that doesn't strike you as odd, but my approach was and has been that if they can't see what I believe from the way I live and conduct myself, what good are my words? I always felt that if you couldn't respect me as a minister from my conduct, don't respect me for the little white collar I wear either.

How close to the original work is what is we read today in English? As I mentioned, I am not a Scripture scholar, but I have no reason to believe that what we read today in English is as close to a faithfully exact translation as scholars can produce. Because of the differences in nuances in languages and customs there is absolutely no doubt in my mind that the most exact meaning of some words, phrases, and expressions cannot be translated perfectly. This may result in not having the exact meaning of what the text intended.

When I began to study Latin, I could never fully understand why the professor told us that some words in foreign languages could not be translated exactly into English. It was only years later when I became proficient in Spanish that I understood what this professor meant.

That is why I am not surprised that scholars still to this day study the lives, language and customs of the Old Testament times to delve into a deeper understanding of the Bible itself.

How should we view the content of the Bible? As the Word of God! If you want to be as sure as you can that you will join Christ in heaven, follow the Bible!

I think I mentioned that you ask some difficult questions, didn't I? Well, to get the full answer to this question, you will need to enroll in a Bible course.

QUESTON #28

I've read of the discovery in the late 1940's of the Dead Sea Scrolls. But, I have heard very little about them in recent years. Do they know when they were written, and what if any relationship they have to the Bible?

RESPONSE #28

You are correct. The Dead Sea Scrolls were discovered between 1947 and 1956. And they shed some light on things we didn't know about the Old Testament prior to that time as a result of this discovery. But in all honesty, I have not kept up to date with any new developments that have resulted from them.

I did research a little online since you asked your question and what I found out is that in December 2007, the Dead Sea Scrolls Foundation commissioned a London publisher to publish exact facsimiles of three scrolls. Of the first three facsimile sets, one was exhibited at the Early Christianity and the Dead Sea Scrolls Exhibition in Seoul, South Korea, and a second set was purchased by the British Library in London.

The Dead Sea scrolls are available online, and can be found with a Web search. They can also be purchased in multi-volumes on disc media or in book form, in certain college and university libraries.

QUSTION #29

If most people of the time of Jesus life on earth were illiterate, and the Apostles and those who were close to Jesus were fishermen or of similar humble background, how did the New Testament get written and when?

RESPONSE #29

I think I touched upon this in the beginning of this Part Three. Though people were illiterate, there were some who could read, write and relate stories. And even those who could not read or write could transmit verbally the stories they heard and most probably did. And who knows what details were omitted or added each time? (You know the game of whispering something orally in a group of ten people? There is always something different when the tenth person hears it.)

The New Testament probably didn't get written until some time after 70 A.D. Matthew and Mark were written about 70 A.D. Luke and the Acts of the Apostles were probably written about 75 A.D. and John, between 90 and 100 A.D. The epistles were written after 50 A.D.

QUESTION #30

Paul seems to have had a great deal of input to the Bible and influence over the foundation of the church. How did he get such insight without ever having known Christ prior to the crucifixion?

RESPONSE #30

Yes, Paul's life and influence in the early Church is quite amazing especially when you consider that he was not one of the Twelve Apostles, never saw Christ in person, and even persecuted the early Christians. But, perhaps, all of this is just to show to what limits God's mercy extends, under what circumstances, and how thorough can be conversion (Acts 9:1–19). As for his insights, remember he was a Pharisee (Act 22:3). Then later he had a supernatural experience and I think we have to accept it as such. The proof of his life-long preaching and endurance of suffering, persecution, and death itself for his faith in Jesus is the proof.

QUESTION #31

Is there any known reason why Christ selected the Apostles? Did they have common characteristics?

RESPONSE #31

I think it would be difficult to determine why Christ selected the Apostles. We have to imagine Him working as a carpenter's son and probably not very busy living in a small village where everyone knew everyone else at least to some degree. The seashore was close and He probably wandered down there often besides attending temple services as the other Jewish people did in His town. The seashore was a busy place since fishing was one of the ways people made a living. After His baptism by John, Jesus first spotted "Simon and his brother Andrew casting their nets...They immediately abandoned their nets and became His followers" (Mark 1: 16-18). He had to have an attractive personality to draw men to Him so quickly. Mark tells us that Jesus "entered the synagogue and began to teach. The people were spellbound by His teaching because He taught with authority, and not like the scribes" (Mark 1:21-22).

All of the Apostles were fishermen, except for Matthew who was a tax collector. Jesus saw something in each one that attracted them to Him. And from the scarce accounts in the New Testament about the apostles, we find very little that shows any common characteristics except for their fishing occupation and willingness to follow Christ.

QUESTION #32

It would seem that the Ten Commandments have had a tremendous influence over the world as we currently know it and perhaps second only to the resurrection of Christ. Do you see that as a reasonable fact?

RESPONSE #32

You make a good observation. I never really thought of it in those terms. Yes, I think that is a safe assumption. I have not traveled much so I can not speak from personal experience, but from my education, reading, and personal acquaintances with others, it seems rather universal that almost everyone is aware of the Ten Commandments and the resurrection of Christ. And for millions of people who do not necessarily profess faith in Christianity, they seem to recognize the existence of a code of ethics that include most of the Ten Commandments...perhaps for some of them, it is not exactly as we know them. But even among non-religious people there seems to be a sense or acquaintance with the Ten Commandments.

QUESTION #33

Exodus 34:6-7 caused me to pause and consider two questions First, it is stated, "The Lord, the Lord, the compassionate and gracious God, slow to anger, abounding in love and faithfulness, maintaining love to thousands, and forgiving wickedness, rebellion and sin". But, then it goes on to state, "yet, he does not leave the guilty unpunished; he punishes the children and their children for the sin of the fathers to the third and fourth generation." I could not help but wonder if that constitutes a contradiction. On one hand God is loving and forgiving and yet he punishes the guilty. Second, would a loving and compassionate God hold the children of the guilty responsible for the sins of their fathers? In addition, is there a reason that the reference is only to the sins of the father and does not mention the mother?

RESPONSE #33

I think your observations are "right on" as they say. You ask, "Is it contradictory?" It certainly is, but I am not sure I know exactly why.

There seems to be a strong sense in the Bible that the children pay for the sins of their father going back to Adam and Eve. Though Eve eats the apple, we speak of "Adam's sin" because he is our father and we inherit through the father supposedly. If a father has riches, he leaves prosperity for his children; if he leaves poverty, then poverty is their inheritance. Thus we have these verses that deal with the father's sins on his children. One observation I read about this issue says that whether or not it is fair to treat the children this way is not the issue. Sin is in the world and the consequences of sin affected many generations.

I say it is contradictory because we find other places in the Bible where God says just the opposite. "Fathers shall not be put to death for their children, nor children for their fathers; only for his own guilt shall a man be put to death" (Deuteronomy 24:16). "Only the one who sins shall die. The son shall not be charged with the guilt of his father, nor shall the father be charged with the guilt of his son. The virtuous man's virtue shall be his own, as the wicked man's wickedness shall be his" (Ezekiel 18:20). And "Come now, let us set things right, says the Lord: Though your sins be like scarlet, they may become white as snow; though they be crimson red, they may become white as wool. If you are willing, and obey, you shall eat the good things of the land;" (Isaiah 1:18-19).

I just want to point out that this concept of the children inheriting their parents' sin was a concept that is referred to in the New Testament. You remember the story of the man born blind in John 9? You will recall that, "His disciples asked Him, 'Rabbi, was it his sin or that of his parents that caused him to be born blind?" (John 9:2)

And the reference only to the sins of the father without mentioning the mother can just be another case of the sexist attitude prevalent at that time against women, or it could be the idea of the father as the sole source of inheritance.

QUESTION #34

In John 14:9-11 Christ speaks of "Don't you believe that I am in the Father, and that the Father is in me? The words I say to you are not just my own. Rather, it is the Father, living in me, who is doing his work. Believe me when I say that I am in the Father and the Father is in me; or at least believe on the evidence of the miracles themselves".

In John 15:4 Christ once again uses the phrase, "remain in me, and I will remain in you".

Had He wanted to, Christ could merely have said, "I'm God". But, He chose to use a more complicated expression. How should we interpret what He meant?

RESPONSE #34

We need only remember how they treated Christ for speaking as He did. Imagine if He had come out and said, "I 'm God." We have to be mindful of Christ's mission to bring mankind to a deeper and better understanding of who God is and what God expects from us. Christ did not come to earth for His own sake; He came to draw all people to the Father. "I came that they might have life and have it to the full" (John 10:10). I wonder if the people would have understood any better if Christ had said, "I'm God!" I think they would have had a very difficult time trying to understand how that was possible. "God? You say you are God! But You are just a human being like the rest of us. "Isn't this the carpenter's sons? Isn't Mary known to be His mother and James, Joseph, Simon, and Judas His brothers? Aren't His sisters our neighbors? Where did He get all this? They found Him altogether too much for them. Jesus said to them, 'No prophet is without honor except in his native place, indeed in his own house.' And He did not work many miracles there because of their lack of faith" (Matthew 13:55-58).

Remember when the unclean spirit shrieked out as Jesus cured a man of a devil? "What do You want of us, Jesus of Nazareth? Have

You come to destroy us? I know who You are – the holy One of God. Jesus rebuked him sharply: Be quiet. Come out of the man" (Mark 1:23-25).

(I need to make this aside: notice the author of Mark has the devil speaking in the plural "us" and then in the next sentence the author has "I". Does that sound familiar when we discussed "Let us make man in our image" in Question Number 13 in Part Three on the Bible?)

I surmise that Christ had no doubt how He would be treated if He came out with "I'm God". He knew how much more difficult it would have been to spread his Father's message of love and forgiveness. It seems from God's plan of the Incarnation of Jesus that stressing the idea that Jesus was God would have defeated the entire purpose of the Incarnation. Jesus already was God and now He became man to show us human beings how human beings should live their lives in order to reach the kingdom of God. If Jesus had pushed the idea that He was God, people could then say, "Hey, that's easy for Him to live like that and follow those commandments and advice because He's God."

How should we interpret what He meant? I can think of no clearer, or more precise explanation than what Jesus Himself tells us in John's Gospel (15:1-8). "I am the true vine and My Father is the vine grower....Live on in Me, as I do in you. No more than a branch can bear fruit of itself apart from the vine can you bear fruit apart from Me. I am the vine, you are the branches. He who lives in Me and I in him, will produce abundantly, for apart from Me you can do nothing. A man/woman who does not live in Me is like a withered, rejected branch, picked up to be thrown in the fire and burnt. If you live in Me, and My words stay part of you, you may ask what you will – it will be done for you."

QUESTION #35

If, as is stated in the Bible, God knew us before we were born, does that imply that he put us on earth at a particular point in time for a specific purpose, and that He also knows when we'll leave our earthly being?

RESPONSE #35

Yes, I think that is precisely what it means. With God – as well as for ourselves, I believe – everything happens for a purpose. Why we were born at this particular time and place may never be known to us, but I believe God has a divine plan for each of us. I'm not speaking about every single little thing that happens to us, but certainly for the major events of our lives. We are His creation and all things were made for Him. "In Him everything in heaven and on earth was created, things visible and invisible, whether thrones or dominations, principalities or powers; all were created through Him, and for Him. He is before all else that is. In Him everything continues in being." (Colossians 1:16-17). And "Through Him all things came into being, and apart from Him nothing came to be. Whatever came to be in Him, found life, life for the light of men" (John 1:3-4).

I can't believe that we were just created to fill the earth and do whatever we please to pass the time. We were meant to be those branches connected to the vine that He speaks about in John's Gospel (15:1-8) and as such to serve a purpose in producing fruit. That is what is behind the idea of knowing one's vocation – a "calling" in life. Each one of us has been given a very different personality and gifts and talents distinct and apart from one another in order to be more readily capable of performing the various tasks in the vineyard of the Lord. And none of us can be absolutely sure of what

God has in store for us. So we need to be conscious of our differences and talents and think about how God may be calling us to work in His vineyard.

I believe that is why God made us male and female – not just for procreation, but to exhibit, display, and utilize those male and female gifts, talents and characteristics that are all various facets of who God is. He is so enormous and awful (full of awe) that no one segment of mankind alone can adequately portray all the attributes of God.

And, therefore, the consequence of this diversity makes it incumbent upon all of us to honor, respect – yes, even love these differences. All of this ties us back into some of the earlier answers I gave above regarding the extent of our inclusiveness as Christians.

QUESTION #36

In the book of Matthew 18:21-35 Jesus speaks of the need to forgive those who sin against us. It's easy to understand and accept forgiveness under the condition that the sinner recognizes his wrong behavior and asks for forgiveness. It's also easy to understand and accept that it's contrary to the spiritual and physical and psychological well being of the person wronged to harbor negative feelings toward someone else. But, it would seem to be much more difficult to forgive someone who continues to believe that they did no wrong, and in fact would do the same ignoble act again. As the level of harm of the sinful act rises, and when it is detrimental to others, so does the difficulty in forgiveness.

As a student of military history, I have pondered what appears to be a conflict between the commandment that we forgive those who have sinned against us and the need to control or prevent those who would kill us or our loved ones, and destroy our culture and values if permitted to do so. There are those who have served in military leadership who claim that it is necessary to dehumanize the enemy, to hate them, and thereby have no qualms about killing them. While that view may well be the opposite of the lesson in Matthew, it has been a thought (and perhaps even a policy) in past wars. Some might even say that it is a necessary element in avoiding the loss of an armed conflict. How should we view this issue?

RESPONSE #36

The scenario that you first describe above about forgiving someone who continues to believe that they did no wrong, and in fact would do the same ignoble act again is either a psychopath, a totally unrepentant sinner, or a confirmed enemy. The psychopath should be excused and put away. The unrepentant sinner needs a moral conversion and probably some serious mental health assistance. The confirmed enemy has to be dealt with as any other enemy. They need to be dealt with as an unjust aggressor since they threaten our very existence as a free, loving, and peaceful people. There is no doubt that as the level of harm of aggression rises for us and others, so will the difficulty of our ability to forgive. That is just pure human nature and not even God would expect us to act differently in these circumstances. There is such a thing called "just anger". Generally, it will be difficult for humans to exercise just anger, but not impossible.

When dealing with an unrepentant enemy as you described, I find no conflict in applying the principles of Christianity. Forgiveness only comes into play – both with God and humans – when the offender is sincerely repentant. No repentance; no forgiveness. Not only are we obligated to use well what God has given us, we must also protect what God has given us. It is difficult to forgive those who seek to destroy us or our way of life. When a person is unjustly attacked, it is not the time to turn the other cheek. We have an obligation to defend ourselves, just as we would go to the defense of someone else under an unjust attack. A sin of omission can be just as serious, or more so as a sin of commission.,

Our country must work very hard to avoid any kind of war, but we would be most naïve to think that there are not people who would love to destroy us. In these circumstances we must be prepared to save and protect the lives that God has entrusted to our country's leaders.

Theology has always taught us of our obligation to protect ourselves against an unjust aggressor, often referred to as self-defense. Based on this principle, theologians have developed a morally legitimate doctrine of a "just war".

You say that there are those who have served in military leadership who claim that it is necessary to dehumanize the enemy, to hate them, and thereby have no qualms about killing them. And that some might even say that it is a necessary element in avoiding the loss of an armed conflict. Whether that is a fact or a way to gain acceptance of that idea, an individual soldier would have to accept that proposition unless He was willing to face court marital, I would presume. Again, I don't want to cop out, but could not that soldier recall the words of Christ, "...to Caesar, what is Caesar's..."(Matthew 22:21). At any rate, certainly treating prisoners of war inhumanely is not only morally wrong; it is against the Geneva Convention, if I am correct.

I think that those who make those claims and decisions must make sure they are on solid ground because they are dealing with human lives. If that is their honest opinion, that is how they will be judged. War is ugly and so are some of the decisions that our leaders have to make. I trust they do not make these decisions without serious thought and, hopefully, prayer for guidance.

As a military person you understand very well the absolute need to defend one's self, one's country, one's values, one's well being. In my opinion, you are probably rare among the military establishment to weigh this obligation against your Christian beliefs, and for this I commend you. We owe the deepest of gratitude to all our military personnel who have sacrificed themselves for our freedom and liberty. I believe the words of Christ "There is no greater love than this: to lay down one's life for one's friends" (John 15:13) rightfully applies to every one of our military men and women.

War may seem contrary to the Gospel message of love of neighbor, but we must remember that love of neighbor does not mean that we have to turn the other cheek if someone abuses us. Sins of omission may be as evil as sins of commission. In fact, the lesson of love extends to protecting what is noble, sacred, and holy – those gifts of God. The Gospel message of loving our neighbor includes not letting ourselves be abused nor surrender our God-given rights of life, liberty, and happiness to unjust aggressors either as individuals or as a community.

QUESTION #37

In James 2:10 it is stated that "For whoever keeps the whole law but fails in one point has become guilty of all of it." Is that a standard that is almost impossible for humans to meet?

RESPONSE #37

I think if you just focus in on James 2:10, I can see your reaction as you stated. However, I think we need to read further. "For He who said, 'You shall not commit adultery,' also said, 'You shall not kill.' If therefore you do not commit adultery but do commit murder, you have become a transgressor of the law."

Remember earlier I said, "a sin is a sin, is a sin"? I think that is what James means here. James is urging his readers to be faithful to the law without making any distinction between serious or less serious transgressions.

I also think that his statement is less than accurate by stating that, "For whoever keeps the whole law..." if one fails in keeping any point of the law, that one does NOT keep the whole law. What would your reaction be if James 2:10 read like this, "For whoever fails to keep the law by even just one small point, fails to keep the whole law?" That is how I understand it.

QUESTION #38

I have read that it is believed that the Gospels were most likely written somewhere between 30 and 70 years after the crucifixion. If that's accurate, were they likely authored by someone other than the apostles, Matthew, Mark, Luke, and John?

RESPONSE #38

I think the dates you quote are generally accepted as correct. I don't think that it would have been impossible for the four of them to have written them in that time frame. Even if someone other than those four individuals actually wrote them, the four Evangelists are considered the authors and the source of the information contained within these Gospels. We have to remember too, that these four individuals did not sit down and decide that they were going to write a Gospel of Jesus Christ..

In order to provide you with more detail regarding the authorship of the four Gospels, I am including information from the "The New American Bible" below for all four Gospels.

Matthew:

Church history tells us that a bishop named Papias in Phrygia who died about 135 A.D., "wrote that Matthew had compiled a collection of sayings of the Lord in the Hebrew tongue (most likely Aramaic), and each person translated them as he was able. This seems to indicate that various Greek versions of the early collection attributed to Matthew were in existence;...And it is probable that the author of Matthew had access to the present gospel of Mark. Matthew is obviously an expanded version of Mark, considered the first gospel form to be written." "Current and more common opinion dates the composition of the gospel of Matthew between 80-100 A.D., or roughly, 85 A.D." (The New American Bible)

Mark:

"According to Papias...the author of the second gospel was Mark who served as Peter's 'interpreter'...There is no need to reject the identification of the author with that John Mark whom the New Testament associated with St. Paul...and with St. Peter..." (The New American Bible)

Luke:

"Most scholars agree that Luke made use of Mark's gospel as one of his sources; some even consider it to be Luke's principal source, to which he added other material...including an independently derived passion-narrative. In the view of others, Luke used Mark only as a supplementary source of rounding out the material he took from other traditions. Certainly, Luke's aim was not to improve upon Mark's account of the public ministry of Jesus, but rather to provide material for those like Theophilus, God's friends,...Early Christian tradition ascribes the companion volumes of the Lucan gospel and Acts of the Apostles to approximately 75 A.D. and identifies the author with Luke the physician, friend of St. Paul..." (The New American Bible)

John:

"The reputed author of the fourth gospel was John, son of Zebedee, who published it at Ephesus in the last years of his life. Within the Christian community, this is the only important tradition that has come down from antiquity concerning this gospel. In its essentials the tradition is found in Irenaeus... toward the close of the second century. He claims to have had it from Polycarp of Smyrna, who knew John. Thus 'the beloved disciple' himself becomes identified as the source of the tradition."

"While the attestation of this tradition is impressive, it should be remembered that for the ancients authorship was a much broader concept than it is today. In their time a man could be called the "author" of a work if he was the authority behind it, even though he did not write it. Modern critical analysis makes it difficult to accept the idea that the gospel as it now stands was written by one man."

A theory proposes "that it was one of John's disciples who actually developed the tradition into the pattern of the gospel as we know it. Perhaps, under John's guidance this disciple was the real evangelist: an artistic and theological genius, who gave to the tradition the distinctive literary feature which we call "Johannine," and who used the gospel message to respond to the pressing theological needs of his time."

"Later, the theory continues, still another disciple of John was responsible for the editing of the evangelist's original gospel. He is often called the disciple-redactor, or editor, to distinguish him from the disciple-evangelist. This man added other material which had come down from the wide circle of Johannine disciples...and seems to have included a large body of material from the disciple-evangelist which had not been incorporated into the original edition of the gospel."

"The final editing of the gospel and arrangement in its present form probably dates between A.D. 90 and 100. Ephesus is still favored by most scholars as the place of composition, though some have proposed the Syrian city of Antioch." (The New American Bible)

QUESTION #39

While the Bible is the definitive source of the life of Christ while on earth, it seems to me that the effect that His life, teaching, and resurrection has had on the world over the past two thousand plus years is also of great significance to all Christians. His living presence today through the Holy Spirit is evidence enough to warrant our faith, commitment and devotion. How should we view the history as seen in the Bible along with the impact that He has had on the world over the past two thousand years?

RESPONSE #39

I don't think that we can view the history as seen in the Bible with the impact that Christ has had on the world in any other way except "ASTOUNDING." It reminds me of the piece "One Solitary Life" which reads like this (I don't know the author) "...He never wrote a book; never held office; never went to college; never visited a big city; never travelled more than two hundred miles from where he was born...He was nailed to a cross between two thieves...while dying, they gambled for his clothing the only property he had on earth...When he was dead he was laid in a borrowed grave...Nineteen centuries have come and gone, and today Jesus is the central figure of the human race; and the leader of mankind's progress. All the armies that have ever marched; all the navies that have ever sailed; all the parliaments that have ever sat; all the kings that ever reigned put together have not affected the life of mankind on earth as powerfully as that one solitary life."

That sort of says it all and very well!

The only thing that anyone of us can add to that is all that He has done for us personally...the many graces and blessings that He has bestowed upon each of us and our loved ones; the thousands of times He has protected us when we were in danger; the thousand times He has pardoned us when we have failed Him and our sisters and brothers; the times we were lost and didn't know where to turn; the times He took our hand and led us out of confusion; and a million other times too numerous to count when He cared for us more than we even cared for ourselves or deserved.

QUESTION #40

While I think that I understand the intent of the statement in Ecclesiastes 1:9, "What has been is what will be, and what has been done is what will be done; there is nothing new under the sun." But, if taken literally (as some people are prone to do with various passages in the Bible) it could cause some to believe that we should be content to live in caves, when in reality not all advances in science or quality of life are negative. Is this an example of how it is important to avoid drawing too much out of the exact words in the Bible without knowing the intent?

RESPONSE #40

As most of the Book of Ecclesiastes says, "nothing is new under the sun". The author of Ecclesiastes is true to his theme "everything is vanity". The only comment I can make regarding your question is that we have to be very, very careful in taking things literally in the Bible. We have to be aware also that sometimes even the authors of the Bible used hyperbole to make a point. Yes, I think this is one good example of seeing too much in the exact words of the Bible.

QUESTION #41

Once again my attention is drawn to what I see as a different view of God when comparing the Old and New Testaments. In the Old Testament, references are made to God's intolerance and anger at those who failed to follow his laws, or who worshiped idols. His response was harsh and devastating. On the other hand, in the New Testament God sent His Son to earth to help guide His people in getting to know Him. Their act in putting Christ on the cross couldn't have been more hurtful, disobedient, disrespectful, and contrary to His will. And yet, God did not strike or destroy those who committed the act as was the case in the Old Testament. What is it that I do not understand? How should I view what I think is not consistent?

RESPONSE #41

Before anything else, Ernie, remember that Christ's purpose for coming to earth was to bridge the insurmountable gap between God and mankind caused by the sin of Adam and Eve. Christ HAD to die to save us!

The Old Testament showed us human beings interpreting the laws of God in accordance with their own culture, times, and traditions. They were not accustomed to showing kindness, forgiveness and understanding and so their personalities were formed by the kind of justice of an eye for an eye and tooth for a tooth that they believed in and by which they lived their lives. They were prone to act that way and even though their priests and rabbis were their spiritual leaders, remember, their whole entire lives – every aspect of it – was intertwined and governed by their spiritual leaders. I would imagine that Iran today is very similar to the way life was for those living in the Old Testament times. (At least that is the impression I draw from what I hear of Iran.) The civil and religious authorities are almost undivided and their religious beliefs affect their lives to almost the smallest detail of daily living.

Christ came to show us the way to the Father and gave us the freedom of the sons and daughters of God. He came to show us mercy and forgiveness. He taught us how to forgive and stressed that the most important thing in life was to love God and one's neighbor. His entire public life was spent driving that lesson home to us with story after story and deed after deed as we have discussed in these questions and responses.

I don't think there is anything here that you don't understand. I think it's a matter of keeping your focus on the New Testament as the fulfillment of God's plan for humanity. With that plan came love, mercy and forgiveness shown to us by a loving, merciful, and forgiving God. Christ said, "Do not think that I have come to abolish the law and the prophets, I have come, not to abolish them, but to fulfill them" (Matthew 5:17). I see Christ's humility, His kindness, forgiveness, gentleness, understanding, care, sympathy, and empathy – and every other virtue as the fulfillment of the law. He continually teaches us showing the way to the Father through a love that only a God could show.

QUESTION #42

While I have not verified it, somewhere in my readings I got the impression that Judas Iscariot was (prior to the crucifixion) personally the closest apostle to Christ. If true, is there a connection with his selling out of Jesus and the ultimate sacrifice that was to be paid for the sins of the world? How can we understand Judas and his act?

RESPONSE #42

A few years ago a magazine published an article saying that they had discovered the "Gospel of Judas" and they made the claim that you mentioned of Judas being Christ's truest apostle from the Judas find. I've heard it mentioned that since Judas was known as the treasurer and is depicted in the last supper as holding a money bag, the other Apostles did not become suspicious when Christ told him to do whatever he had to do before the betrayal. If any of them heard Christ tell him that, they may have thought he was going to make a purchase for something they needed.

I don't know how we can fully understand Judas and his act. There are lots of stories about Judas. One is that since he knew that Christ had worked those miracles, he believed that Christ would escape before his enemies could harm him.

Part Four

The Church

THE CHURCH

If there were no Church we'd have to establish one. But, from the beginning Christ saw the need to have a foundation from which His followers could go out into the world and teach the gospel. Among the obvious functions that I believe require the Church are:

- Perpetuation of the teachings of Christ
- Maintaining the integrity of the message
- Providing a central place of worship
- Providing a location for the disciples to administer the sacraments
- Providing for authoritative theological education for those who would serve as "Shepherd's" (priests, pastors, ministers), and leaders of the faith
- To serve as a base for those who would carry the teachings of Christ around the world

In short, without the Church it is not likely that the true message of Christ would continue to be taught as it has been over the past 2000 plus years. While we've seen many groups that continue to split from the original Church over differences in emphasis or theology, if we lacked the organization and structure of the church there would likely be countless more that would sprout up in response to the ideas of currently popular people or changing values and culture.

Most likely, over time, many would also move away from the basic truths of Christianity.

In addition to the above, the church serves as the focal point for the glorification of God. I remember being impressed while visiting in Bermuda to learn that the island was originally settled several hundred years ago by survivors of a British sailing ship that had sunk off its coast. With all their obvious problems and needs, the first order of business for the survivors was to erect a church to acknowledge and glorify God. That action said a great deal about their priorities.

Frank, is there anything you would like to add?

Ernie, I have just three comments. First, when we speak of the "Church" we have to clarify what we mean. The dictionary gives several different meanings for the word. It can mean a building for public worship; a congregation of people; a religious service; a specified Christian denomination; ecclesiastical power as distinguished from secular power; the clerical profession; the company of all Christians regarded as a mystic spiritual body; or the people of God, sometimes referred to 'the assembly' or 'the living stones of the Church'. It is important to keep these distinctions in mind for a logical discussion of the subject.

Second, we must keep in mind what is the main purpose of the Church? While the Church certainly can and should carry out all those functions you mention above, the main purpose of the Church is to lead people to holiness – to God. And that is why whenever a Church or any of its leaders are unfaithful to this primary mission, we, the people of God, are rightly shocked, and surprised. Politicians, teachers, athletes, entertainers, and many other public figures betray the rules of morality and create shock and scandal, but nothing compared to the scandal from a Church or its leaders. That is because the very realm of the Church consists of maintaining the moral order.

Third, the question of one true church often comes up. I don't pretend to be an authority on the subject, but my personal belief is that Christ did not come to establish a "specific religion". He came to show us a better way to the Father. One reason that leads me to believe so is that I do not think there would be so much religious disparity in the world if Christ intended to establish just one true religion. Even if we just look at Christianity today we find a plethora of beliefs concerning God and our relationship to the Divinity. Many of the differences in belief among the various denominations are rather insignificant when we consider the entire picture of God. I think most of those who have seriously attempted to explain God and our relationship with Him and as a result have formed "another religion" have been sincere, honest, and spiritual people seeking God just like everyone else. Some may have protested against one another, but history has shown that many of those protests were not in vain, nor unwarranted to some degree. I'd like to quote Richard Rohr in his book, "*The Naked Now*". "It is amazing arrogance that allows Christians to so readily believe that their mental understanding of things is anywhere close to that of Jesus. Jesus said, 'I am the Way, the Truth, and the Life' (John 14:6). I think the intended effect of that often misused line is this: If Jesus is the Truth, then you probably aren't."

However, my main reason for believing that there is no one true religion is that if Christ commanded us to "love our neighbor as ourselves," He must have certainly followed His own rule Himself!

PART FOUR

THE CHURCH

QUESTIONS

&

RESPONSES

QUESTION #1

It would be easy to come up with a list of factors that have contributed to the growth of Christianity. But, the fact that it's based on Jesus Christ with all its truth and holiness would obviously top the list. In addition, it would be easy to make the argument that the Apostles, the Church and all those who answered His calling over the past 2000 plus years would follow. It's been through the commitment, obedience, hardship, examples, and total dedication of these servants of Christ that the word has been passed. What guidance and encouragement would you give to those lay people who desire to help in carrying forth the message of Christ?

RESPONSE #1

As you know, Ernie, you don't have to be a clergy person, or the president of your church's pastoral council, or even join one of your church's organizations to carry forth the message of Christ. Of course, if you feel called to participate in any of these ways, by all means follow your calling. And even if you don't feel called right now, may be it would be worth looking into participating in different ways later on.

You are familiar with the many different ways you can carry forth Christ's message which besides enhancing your spiritual life will enrich your life in general as you meet more people on different levels of their lives. From your many contacts you already know how wonderful and refreshing it is to meet others with similar interests.

One of my favorite sayings is, "Actions speak louder than words." There are so many who call themselves Christians, but show no actions. And that other saying, "What you are speaks so loudly, I can't hear what you say."

I'm sure you have already discovered that one of the best ways to promote Christ's message and encourage others to follow it, is by living His message to the full yourself. You don't have to preach it; just live your life as a genuine and sincere follower of Christ. By letting others see the joy and happiness in your own daily life, you show what you believe and how deeply you believe it. More than anything else we show this by the way we treat other people. Our treatment of others reflects our attitude towards them. We can't fake it because if we try to, it will only look phony.

QUESTION #2

It is widely acknowledged that each generation tends to bring about changes in values, culture, and priorities. Those of us who now enjoy being grandparents are in awe of many of the achievements of our offspring. But, we have also seen some trends that cause us concern. Among them are the prevalence of illegal drug use, casual sex, a minimizing of the sacrament of marriage, the increase in single parent families, gratuitous violence and immorality in the media, a very high expectation of pleasure and immediate gratification, Should, and is, the Church making an effort to respond to that trend?

RESPONSE #2

Let's clarify what you mean by "Church". Do you mean the individual denominations – Lutheran, Methodist, Episcopalian, Catholic, Presbyterian, etc., etc. (Let's not forget our Jewish brothers and sisters too, as well as Muslims, Buddhists and other Eastern religions.) I am not up to date with what any of these denominations are doing in any specific way to combat the trend that you mention. But my comments to this question sort of ties into my response above.

We – all of us – are the "Church". The people are the Church, but we get so confused with considering the various hierarchies of the different religious faiths and the buildings in which we congregate to praise God as "the Church".

The established religious denominations can make all the rules and regulations that they can devise to attack the trend, but unless we (the people - the true "Church") do something about the trend, nothing will happen, nothing will change.

When our children were in public school, we were advised that the school would be showing a sex education movie and the children needed parental permission to attend. One of the parents told me that he was waiting for our pastor to tell us if we should let our children see the movie. Whose obligation was it, the pastor's or the parents'? Obviously this man did not see himself as "Church".

Society for some time now has lost its sense of shame; its sense of guilt; its sense of decency; its sense of morality; its sense of values; its sense of responsibility; its sense of honesty; its sense of religion; its sense of God. (Did I leave anything out?)

So, I guess I would rephrase your question like this: are we – the faithful making an effort to respond to that trend? If each of us does not see the need, the obligation to address this trend in our positions as members of the Church, as parents, as citizens, as responsible adults, as followers of Christ, then we can be sure there will be no change in the trend. Just as world peace begins with me, so changing society's customs, habits, and standards begins with each one of us too. We must ask ourselves some tough questions like, how do I contribute to this trend? What do I do to combat it from the position I find myself in life? Are there ways that I can contribute more actively to opposing this trend in my own personal life, my family, my circle of friends, etc. Am I doing all that I should?

Could I be accused of not trying hard enough? Do I support any of this trend by viewing it, paying to watch it, buying their products, etc., etc. If we truly see ourselves as "Church", we may understand our obligations in a different light.

I don't want to interject any discussion of politics because this in not the forum for it. However, it is an important area in most people's lives and we need to remember to apply our Christian principles here also in guiding us as we consider the various options and positions presented. As Christians we have an obligation to partake in the political process by voting according to our consciences. We must always remember to be fair, loyal, and honest about the issues and the common good which supersedes the individual good. Sometimes an individual's rights or group of individuals' rights may have to defer to the common good. This isn't always easy to do. Deciding any issue based purely on politics is unfair and definitely unchristian if it offends against the common good of society and the command to love your neighbor.

QUESTION #3

I have a great respect for the liturgy, rituals, and traditions of the Church. They're like the mortar that holds the bricks together. They provide a common understanding and experience to its members, and they communicate and perpetuate our core beliefs. Certainly, the experience of each Christmas and Easter are events that are both anticipated and memorable. Church service on Christmas Eve with "Silent Night" and all that goes with the marking of the birth of Christ has a magical effect on many people throughout the world, and it can't help but to enhance our faith and good will to mankind. Similarly, Easter, with its message of redemption and everlasting life through Christ is a day that brings forth a special understanding for all Christians. Add to that list, baptism, communion, and weekly church services. How do you see these events and special days affecting the lives of those of us who follow Christ?

RESPONSE #3

I am glad to hear how these religious feast days and liturgical celebrations serve to enhance your spiritual life. You are probably in a minority though, sad to say. That is only my opinion. But I say that because statistically from what I heard and read is that Church attendance is declining over the years. And even for those who do attend, many do it out of a sense of "duty" – (For many Catholics, going to church is seen as a way to avoid serious sin; - not a great motive for going.) And then there are so many who go and can't wait to get out. By the time communion comes, the Church is quite empty.

For those who attend weekly services, as obviously you do, as a means of living a deeper spiritual life – seeking to learn more about yourself and your relationship with God – I would definitely encourage continual attendance because you "get something out of going" because "you put something into it". Many people don't go to Church because they say, "I get nothing out of it." From "nothing" you get "nothing" (except if you are God.)

These religious celebrations are meant to revitalize our lives (as in your case) by recalling the special event of each celebration. They are reminders of our lives of faith and the extent to which God loves us. We need these constant reminders to refresh our faith and deepen our love and gratitude for these gifts. These special religious days are like our national holidays when we celebrate the lives of our past leaders, special events in our history, or our veterans who gave their lives for our freedom.

Liturgical events - we remember...we celebrate...we believe!

QUESTION #4

As I look at Christianity today I see it in three parts – God, the Church which carries on the teachings of Christ, and the people (the children of God). Without the church binding the two parts together it would be difficult to conceive how we could continue to carry the message to future generations. So, I'm convinced of the absolute need to maintain a strong church with a solid and practical aspect that enables it to withstand the constant non-Christian social trends. But, as we have seen in recent years, the leaders of the church (all denominations) are human and subject to all the temptations of the world. When a shepherd fails to meet his responsibilities the sheep stray and get lost. Hopefully God's hand will be upon those who have answered His call, but what if anything can, or should, be done to maintain the credibility and respect for those who lead us?

RESPONSE #4

Another tough question, but extremely relevant and very important!

No question that it is very hypocritical when we see anyone in any kind of position of moral authority – church leader, clergy person, politician, scout leader, teacher, coach, etc. – involved in any kind of scandal. And of late, the revelations of so many involved in sexual scandals gives us all much to ponder. These scandals cause more serious problems for us because these people freely put themselves forward as leaders.

You didn't mention forgiveness for those involved in these situations, but I presume that is because you know the answer is that we must forgive them. Forgiving does not mean forgetting and dismissing the penalties and consequences of irresponsibility.

One of my classmates who is still in the active ministry and a very good priest told us that it is difficult to walk down the street in a Roman collar today because one does not know what is going through the mind of the people who see him.

But I think we have to be very non-judgmental about the clergy. Remember, "If you want to avoid judgment, stop passing judgment." (Matthew 7:1) We have to be very considerate of our leaders always remembering that they are just as human as we are. My mother never liked to hear us talk about the nuns who taught us in school. And if we said something negative about one of them, my Mother would say, "She had her faults before she went to the convent, and she took them with her."

Treat our leaders with the respect their position deserves and if you have no reason to suspect them of misconduct, don't scrutinize them. Treat them as you would treat anyone else. If your particular minister, clergyman is open to it, why not try to engage him in a discussion of the topic. It may prove to be an enlightening experience to hear how he conducts his life in light of the subject.

QUESTION #5

We increasingly hear more about the need to have tolerance and acceptance of other religions. Given the fact that all people are the children of God, it makes sense to extend love and compassion to everyone. But, since some religions advocate beliefs that are in conflict with the tenets of Christianity is it reasonable and right to accept those ideologies?

RESPONSE #5

We must always distinguish between the messenger and the message; the doer and the deed. They are not the same and we shouldn't treat them the same. Again, we are commanded to love the messenger, the doer; there is no command regarding the message or the deed.

Must we accept those ideologies? No more than we need to accept anything else with which we disagree. Just because these beliefs may be "religious" in nature, it doesn't follow that we have to accept any of them. In fact, depending on which ones they are, we probably have to reject them because they may run contrary to our own religious beliefs. "No man/woman can serve two masters." (Matthew 6:24).

QUESTION #6

The Church occupies an indispensible role in the leadership of the Christian world. Without that educated, committed, and ordained body we would lack standards, truth, and the ability to work together as brothers and sisters in Christ. However, mass communication has tended to focus us upon serious social issues that were always present but just not communicated as they are today. In response, there has been a tendency among some denominations to reflect the current culture, and to yield to public opinion rather than to maintain the values contained in the Bible. There is a rationalizing of behavior, the avoidance of inconvenience, justifying the desire of people for pleasure, comfort, and material well being of their congregation, and an acceptance of the trend to individual freedom to establish your own value structure. In addition, there is an increasing tendency to challenge the authority of the Church. Among these issues are abortion, minimizing the importance of a commitment in marriage;

lust for personal power; greed; and the list goes on and on. Is this truly a trend that is detrimental to Christianity? If that is a fair observation, is the Church showing adequate leadership as a shepherd should?

RESPONSE #6

By all means this is a trend that is very detrimental to Christianity because it preaches an entirely contrary message.

You paint a pretty accurate picture of what "the people of God" (read "Church") face today. This "mass communication" you speak about can easily be termed "the world" as referred to in your Question 43 in Part Three. It could also be referred to as the "wolves in sheep clothing" "Be on your guard against false prophets, who come to you in sheep's clothing, but underneath are wolves on the prowl. You will know them by their deeds." (Matthew 7:15-16)

Paul counsels us against this mass media: "Do not conform yourselves to this age but be transformed by the renewal of your mind, so that you may judge what is God's will, what is good, pleasing and perfect" (Romans 12:2).

And Christ prays for His disciples and followers' protection while they struggle on earth in His prayer to the Father. "...They do not belong to the world [any more than I belong to the world]. I do not ask You to take them out of the world, but to guard them from the evil one. They are not of the world, any more than I belong to the world" (John 17: 14-16).

Yes, this vicious, subtle attack – almost like a hidden cancer to those unaware by their lack of interest in things spiritual – spreads itself very easily because it is like living on "Easy Street". Christ warned us that following Him wasn't living on Easy Street. If we want to follow Him He said, "If anyone wishes to come after Me, He must deny himself, take up his cross and follow in My steps" (Mark 8:34). "Enter through the narrow gate. The gate that leads to damnation is wide, the road is clear, and many choose to travel it. But how narrow is the gate that leads to life, how rough the road, and how few there are who find it" (Matthew 7:13-14).

You ask if the Church is showing adequate leadership as a shepherd should regarding this trend. We already explained above what we mean by "Church". I would just repeat here that both the Church faithful and the Church leadership have a serious obligation to oppose this trend in our daily lives and with the same enthusiasm and passion that we pursue our natural lives as discussed above. If we are true followers of Christ, we have to follow, support and be guided by Christ's entire message – both the easy parts as well as the more difficult parts of His message. Churches must do the same. "That is why whoever breaks the least significant of these commands and teaches others to do so shall be called least in the kingdom of God...I tell you, unless your holiness surpasses that of the scribes and Pharisees you shall not enter the kingdom of God" (Matthew 5:19:21).

For those denominations who reflect the current culture and yield to public opinion rather than maintain the values of the Bible, perhaps they may be some of those whom Christ referred to as "wolves in sheep clothing".

QUESTION #7

Having raised the question of commitment by the flock, it would be hard to ignore the damage done by pastors across the spectrum of the Christian Church who failed to live up to their responsibilities. Most people recognize that this group represents a small percentage of the total. But, as so often happens when some fail, it has a negative effect on the entire organization. Is the Church dealing with this problem in a reasonable and effective manner, and consistent with the obligation for obedience, but tempered with forgiveness and grace?

RESPONSE #7

While Christ had His Judas and all professions have had theirs also, it is no excuse for the sins, crimes, abuse, scandal, injustices and harm that have resulted from the damage done by pastors to their people across the spectrum of Christianity. You are absolutely correct in observing how such conduct can have a disastrous effect on the entire organization.

We read in the Old Testament, "Woe to the shepherds who mislead and scatter the flock of my pasture, says the Lord...You have scattered my sheep and driven them away. You have not cared for them, but I will take care to punish your evil deeds..." (Jeremiah 23:1-2). "Woe to my foolish shepherd who forsakes the flock. May the sword fall upon his arm and upon his right eye; let his arm wither away entirely, and his right eye be blinded forever" (Zechariah 11: 17). Pretty strong words, but remember, it's the Old Testament!

More apropos to the situation is Christ's words about avoiding scandal: "Whoever welcomes one such child for my sake, welcomes Me. On the other hand, it would be better for anyone who leads astray one of these little ones who believe in Me, to be drowned by a millstone around His neck, in the depths of the sea. What terrible things will come on the world through scandal. It is inevitable that scandal should occur. Nonetheless, woe to that man through whom scandal comes. If your hand or foot is your undoing, cut it off and throw it from you. Better to enter life maimed or crippled than be thrown with two hands or two feet into endless fire. If your eye is your downfall, gouge it out and cast it from you. Better to enter life with one eye than be thrown with both into fiery Gehenna. See that you never despise one of these little ones. I assure you, their angels in heaven constantly behold My heavenly Father's face" (Matthew 18: 5-10). I want to point out here that we should not use this text to sanction maiming ourselves. It should be understood in a hyperbolic sense meaning that such a one needs some very serious attention for a remedy.

How is the Church dealing with the problem? I heard a commentator say, and I believe it, that this current scandal in the Catholic Church is the most serious crisis the Church has found herself in during modern times. If ever the Church needed the Holy Spirit's guidance, now is the time. I am not in a position to determine how well the Church is dealing with the problem or how effective her course will be. I know that there is deep discord and deep dissatisfaction with what has been done to date. That indicates to me that many, many of the faithful and many clergy themselves are dissatisfied with the way the crisis has been handled so far. Though I can understand how the situation reached the stage at which it is now, I do not believe that the Church authorities handled the situation as well as it could and should have. There is much blame to be shared by all.

QUESTION #8

Attending church services has the obvious function of enabling us to praise the Lord in the company of our brothers and sisters in Christ. It helps rejuvenate our soul much like a car needs to be refilled with gas. But, the Church goes beyond filling personal needs. It also serves as the foundation of our beliefs and enables their perpetuation to future generations. And, it of course, enables us as individuals to join together with other Christians in carrying the message of Christ to the world in practical terms. But, I suppose those benefits are the obvious ones. How should we as Christians look upon the Church, the faithfulness of attendance, and our support?

RESPONSE #8

I think you know how I view "Church". But I think you mean "Church" here as "an organizational entity" surely made up of people, but still something apart from the individuals themselves. That is my approach here.

The Church in this sense needs our support in the form of "time, talent, and treasure". The Church, therefore, must be the most important place where its members can find its roots. This must be the shinning example of what Christianity is all about.

TIME: I believe that a member of an organized Church should seriously consider finding time to serve in some capacity in ministry actively participating in the liturgy as a deacon, lector, Eucharistic minister, server, choir member, usher, greeter, etc. If one does not feel called to that kind of participation, there are needs outside of liturgy or Church services where one can serve in some administrative or social capacity – secretary, treasurer, or heading up or serving on one of the many Church committees in various ways. The idea is to be of service using the God-given talents for the good of the community.

TALENT: Together with time comes your various talents. One needs to review all the activities of the Church to see how and where he can serve. We should always remember that our gifts are not given to us for ourselves as much as they are given to us for service to others.

TREASURE: Every Church has financial needs not only for the salaries of those who are working full-time for the Church "for the laborer is worth his wages" (Luke 10:7), but also for the upkeep of the facility including utilities and rent, etc., etc. But also Churches run programs for the members and do outreach to groups that are in need to carry out its mission of the corporal works of mercy. These need financial support and the members should seriously consider their ability to contribute on a regular basis so that the Church can properly plan and organize its programs. I know that some denominations require tithing; Catholics do not. My only comment on this is that each person knows his circumstances and should feel completely free to give according to one's need. If someone is struggling to pay the rent and a certain amount has been determined as that person's contribution to the Church, it could become a hardship for that person. There is an old saying, "Charity begins at home." I think the Gospel story of the widow's mite also helps us to understand our contributions to the church. "He glanced up and saw the rich putting their offerings into the treasury, and also a poor widow putting in two copper coins. At that He said: 'I assure you, this poor widow has put in more than all the rest. They make contributions out of their surplus, but she from her want has given what she could not afford-every penny she had to live on" (Luke 21:1-4). Our contributions to the Church are supposed to be a "free will offering".

QUESTION #9

I have heard that some Christian Churches prohibit music in their services. While I would agree that nothing, including music, should interfere with the reverence in glorifying God, music is somewhat like an international language and can be very inspiring. When I participate in the singing of classics such as, "How Great Thou Art", or "Silent Night", it is a moving and spiritual experience. Is there anything in the scriptures that addresses the issue of using music in a service?

RESPONSE #9

I know of no place in the Bible that supports a prohibition of music in church services. Music has always been a part of divine worship. St. Benedict says that singing is praying twice.

In the Old Testament we read, "Sing to the Lord, all the earth,.."
(1Chronicles 16:23). And "Then David, girt with a linen apron, came dancing before the Lord with abandon, as he and all the Israelites were bringing up the ark of the Lord with shouts of joy and to the sound of the horn." (2 Samuel 6:14-15).

QUESTION #10

I have heard the statement attributed to Christ, "My kingdom is not of this world". How does the Church view its influence in balancing the moral behavior of people with secular governments and values?

RESPONSE #10

I believe that the Church is well aware of its moral obligation for the most part. I say, "for the most part," because some denominations will stay clear of a secular issue for various reasons. It is not beyond some Churches to avoid a controversy with the civil authorities, or refrain from commenting, because the church may feel it is not politically correct or speaking out could hurt its status as a private non-profit entity. We have to remember that the Churches are headed up by human beings some of whom may be less astute and serious about their spiritual message if there is any danger of being seen in opposition to the "powers that are". It has not been unheard of to have ordained ministers also holding political office. I believe there are a few at this present time who are members of Congress.

Some Churches will take a stand on some moral issues while avoiding other moral issues which they feel are not as important or relevant to the majority of their people. The lack of consistency in Church politics should not surprise us since human beings are involved. Again, I would refer the reader to my response Number 2 in this Part about the proper attitude of Christians toward politics.

QUESTION #11

The United States is primarily a Christian country, with Protestants and Catholics being the dominate denominations. But, the Eastern Orthodox Church has early and deep roots that played a major role in perpetuating Christianity. How, if at all, does the Eastern Orthodox Church differ from the Protestant and Catholic faiths?

RESPONSE #11

I am sorry to disappoint you, Ernie, but I know very little about the Eastern Orthodox Church and could not even attempt to answer your question. The one difference that I am well aware of is that the Eastern Orthodox allows their bishops and priests to marry as long as it is done before ordination, I believe. As you know, the Eastern Orthodox Church is not in union with the Roman Catholic Church, but there is a branch of the Eastern Catholic Church that is in union with Rome. So a Catholic may attend the Western or Eastern Catholic Church.

QUESTION #12

Most Christians have heard of Constantine, Thomas Aquinas, Saint Augustine, and Saint Francis of Assisi and Martin Luther and something of their influence in shaping the Church. Who would you say are among those few who warrant special recognition for bringing forth the teachings of Christ and establishing the Church?

RESPONSE #12

I wouldn't exclude anyone whom you have already mentioned, but I would add all the Apostles (with special mention to the four evangelists) and Paul since they were the first to preach Christ. I'd add Benedict (for his contributions on monasticism), Thomas Aquinas (for influence in theology), John Wesley, John Calvin, John Wycliffe, Thomas More, Francis Xavier, Theresa of Avila, Vincent DePaul and Ignatius of Loyola (founder of the Jesuits). There certainly are more, but it depends on how long of a list you want.

QUESTION #13

Are the similarities of the major Christian denominations greater than their differences?

RESPONSE #13

I would think that the similarities of the major Christian denominations are greater than their differences. The problem for many is that they focus on the differences too frequently and forget about the similarities. (As an aside I would add that many of us do the same thing in our views on race and ethnic origins. We see the few differences and never even consider any similarities.) They are called "Christian" because they all believe in Christ and supposedly follow His teachings. One area of differences is how each denomination interprets His teachings, i.e., which ones are the important issues, and how are these issues defined and explained as relative to our own lives. Of course, the liturgies and church services held in each denomination also vary. In the past we could generally say that Protestant denominations tended to place more emphasis on the Word of God and preaching, where as the Catholic Church emphasized liturgical services over preaching. Since the Second Vatican Council, the Catholic Church has placed more emphasis on preaching while not diminishing the importance of the liturgy.

QUESTION #14

There are current statistics pointing to the fact that the growth of Christianity is greater in Africa and South America than in the United States or Europe. In addition, there are some reports that indicate that in the United States and South America the movement is leaning toward the evangelical churches. Are those reported trends accurate, and if they are, to what would you attribute them?

RESPONSE #14

I have heard of the same reports that you mention and apparently this has been the trend for many years of late. I can not attest to the accuracy of those reports, but I have not heard anything that contradicts them.

If this is true, I am not sure what attributes to this increase. Although the Catholic Church promotes humanitarian aid as part of its overall mission, I am not sure to what extent this is done in Africa and South America compared to the efforts of the evangelical churches. While in the Dominican Republic, our parish ran food, clothing, and medicine programs for the people. In addition, we established work programs where we provided families with food in return for labor on building schools, roads, bridges, and other community projects. We probably served more people through these programs than we did through our Church services. I justified this involvement from words by Pope Pius XII who said, "If you speak to a hungry man about Christ, he will be listening more to his stomach than to you. First feed him, then speak to him about God."

As you know, there is tremendous poverty in these countries and it should come as no surprise that any group that addresses the need for food, clothing, medicine, and shelter will gather many more than if you just address their spiritual needs. I am not sure to what extent evangelicals expend resources to address the material needs of these people.

But there is also another element, in my opinion. I believe Catholicism's form of worship is somewhat less appealing to many of these people who have learned to celebrate in a livelier environment. The first mass celebration of my Virgin Island classmate was by far much more emotional and celebratory than was mine in Buffalo, New York.

QUESTION #15

Are the words in the Apostle's Creed, "---is seated at the right hand of the Father" in conflict with the trilogy (Father, Son, and Holy Ghost) being one?

RESPONSE #15

I see no conflict with the words in the Apostle's Creed and the trilogy of Father, Son, and Holy Spirit being one. My reasoning is this: no human can understand the Blessed Trinity. To our dualistic mind, it is inconceivable how there can be three equal and distinct persons in one God. It is a mystery that we accept on faith.

There are many matters of faith that we cannot understand because we see things only as one way or the other, yet there may be another way to see and understand things that are foreign to us. Look at the animal kingdom. How is it that certain dogs can be trained to become Seeing Eye dogs and know when it's safe to cross a street and how to take its owner to work? Monkeys can become the eyes and hands of its owner. Animals of different species can almost act like humans in caring for one another. If these things are possible in the realm of animals that we know, why is it not possible that things of the supernatural and spiritual world may also be true yet beyond our comprehension? We may not be able to explain them, but that doesn't mean they can not be so.

Perhaps, I have gone somewhat astray with my response, and should have limited it to what I learned about this expression, namely, that "...is seated at the right hand of the Father" means that Christ is said to sit at the right hand of the Father in as much as He reigns together with the Father, and has judiciary power from Him.

QUESTION #16

We tend to look at Christianity as the period during which Christ was on earth, followed by the period when the Church was getting established, and also the current time. But, there was that long period between the early Church and now, (including the Crusades) and it wasn't always an enlightened time. How should we view that period?

RESPONSE #16

It is absolutely amazing when one realizes that there were eight or nine Crusades that lasted for 200 years. To give a perspective on how long that is, just remember that our country is just about that old... My goodness! What was so important that religions, mind you, not the civil government, the Church was conducting these wars... and for what? To deliver the Holy Places from non-believers!

I remember reading that some historians believe that the Crusades were the single most important series of events in the Middle Ages. They say that the significant changes that took place in the structure of European society in the 12th and 13th centuries were considered to be the direct result of Europe's participation in the Crusades. That isn't held today as true. They believe there were many other contributing factors during this time.

The Crusades were responsible for many changes in Europe. The armies that were formed and the supplies needed for Crusaders stimulated the economy. There was a lot of interaction between the East and West which affected European culture in the arts, architecture, literature, and education. They even attribute the pope's vision of directing the energies of the warring knights outside of Europe to have reduced war within Europe.

While I have learned not to judge the past by today's norms and manner of thinking, it is difficult for me to fully understand how the Catholic Church could have waged bloody wars in which thousands of people died for the purpose of possessing land that was considered sacred. To me, one single life is not worth all the sacred lands in the Holy Land together. It seems unbelievable that during those two hundred years there was no one of all those dedicated Christians who could have proposed to end the conflict sooner. We scoff at the Irish of Northern Ireland for their endless religious war. Were not the Crusades just as terrible or worse?

How should we view that period? It was an opportunity to spread Christianity at the terrible price of war and deaths of thousands of people. Since we are so far removed from that period, it behooves us to be very charitable in rushing to judge those responsible for these wars because we know of Christ command not to judge others. And as always, we must forgive them for any injustices, yes, and even the deaths caused by their actions even though done in the name of God.

Epilogue

My walk down the road in recent years in search of an understanding of the Bible, and increased faith in our Lord has largely been an effort in reading, listening to others, and trying to absorb, digest, and analyze Christianity from what is known, and what is believed by those who know more than I.

The experience over the past months while working with my co-author, and good friend, Frank Hoerner, has helped to bring into focus the many questions that had been on my mind. I'm still a very long way from being more than a student of Christianity. And, I'm resolved to the fact that I will not live long enough to reach the point where I can say that I am all that a Christian should be, but there can be no doubt that each day is a tiny bit in the move forward.

One of the more important things that I've learned is that Christ lives today, and through the Holy Spirit He is our compass, and our focus on the true purpose of life.

I doubt that there are many questions in this document that had not previously been thought by others. But, hopefully the answers that Frank has provided will be as enlightening to them as they have been to me.

In addition to the instructive nature of this book, it is my hope that those who read it will see it as an example of not having to be reluctant or inhibited in expressing or discussing their relationship with God. No matter what our age or our position in life, we're all God's children, and learning what that means is a life long pursuit.

And your final words, Frank...

I believe that "creation" is God's relationship to us; and "religion" is our relationship to God! And I do not believe that belonging to a particular religion, or not belonging to one, will save or condemn anyone! Strange coming from a minister, huh?

Upon meeting our Creator, I don't hear Him asking any of us to what religion we belonged on earth, or who was our pastor, or even how often we went to church! No, I think we will hear one question: "Did you live your life the way I revealed myself to YOU?" And no one can answer that question for you except yourself! You can't point to me and say, "Uh...Frank told me to..." nor can I point to you and say "But I listened to Ernie and he said...."

*Our God has told us what the answer must be...LOVE of God and LOVE of each other, but <u>unconditional</u> love! He shows us what unconditional means. "If you bring your gift to the altar and there recall that your brother or sister has anything against you, leave your gift at the altar, go first to be reconciled with your brother or sister and then come and offer your gift" (Matthew 5:23-24). Look closely at this! He doesn't say "if **you** have something against your sister or brother". No, he says, if you remember that **YOUR sister or brother has anything against you,** leave your gift and FIRST before anything else, make up with him or her, tell her or him that YOU are sorry that she or he is mad at you! And he doesn't tell you to argue about it or explain anything – just do it!!!*

Is this easy? If it were easy, would Christ have to remind us so many times that His message is very simple? It's all about love of God and others. He didn't say it was easy; He said it was His command!

We can go to Church and read our Bibles every day of the week! We can do the noblest of deeds and write the greatest of books! We can give away all or earthly possessions and work until we drop; we can...hey, ...just turn to St. Paul and listen to him...

"Now I will show you the way which surpasses all the others. If I speak with human tongues and angelic as well, but do not have love, I am a noisy gong, a clanging cymbal. If I have the gift of prophecy and, with full knowledge, comprehend all mysteries, if I have faith great enough to move mountains, but have not love, I am nothing. If I give everything I have to the feed the poor and hand over my body to be burned, but have not love, I gain nothing. Love is patient; love is kind. Love is not jealous, it does not put on airs, is not snobbish. Love is never rude, it is not self-seeking, it is not prone to anger; neither does it brood over injuries. Love does not rejoice in what is wrong, but rejoices with the truth. There is no limit to love's forbearance, to its trust, its hope, its power to endure. Love never fails... There are in the end three things that last: faith, hope, and love, and the greatest of these is love" (1Corinthians 13:1-13).